Enthusiastic *You!*

Rediscover Your Passion & Energy:
Tools For Success in Your Daily Life

by Joshua M. Evans

Hello Doris!

Please enjoy this book!
I hope it help's you to reclaim
your passion for the work you do!

Enthusiastically,

©2015 Joshua M. Evans

Houston, TX

josh@enthusiasticyou.com

Publisher:

Elite Online Publishing

63 East 11400 South Suite #230

Sandy, UT 84070

ISBN-13: 978-1519633057

ISBN-10: 151963305X

Register This book and get free updates.

Things change rapidly in the publishing world! If you register your copy of this book, we will keep you up to date about this book. PLUS, we will send you an Enthusiastic Checklist PDF.

Just visit http://enthusiasticyoubook.com

Dedicated to:

My lovely wife Sophia, nothing would be possible without your love and support, and to Luke, may your life be filled with countless adventures and immeasurable enthusiasm!

About the author

Joshua M. Evans is the founder of Enthusiastic You!, a motivational consulting and sales training organization headquartered in Houston, Texas.

Growing up just outside of Houston, Joshua's personality and enthusiasm led him quickly into professional sales, where he honed his talent and built his business. After entering professional sales, Joshua soon became aware that his natural passion and enthusiasm were rare but welcome commodities in the companies who hired him.

Since discovering both the power and the scarcity of enthusiasm, Joshua has made it his mission to incite enthusiasm in others, and he founded Enthusiastic You! to help him achieve this goal. Using his proprietary tools and methods, Joshua helps his clients become more enthusiastic in both their business and everyday lives. Joshua feels that everyone can become passionate and unapologetically enthusiastic, and he has dedicated himself to bringing the benefits of enthusiasm to every client he serves.

He enjoys spending time with his wife and son. He spends his spare time sailing, skiing, and playing guitar.

Table Of Contents

FOREWARD

by Susan Casias,

CEO/Founder of The Sales Energizer

I met Josh over 10 years ago when I hired him. He soon became one of our top sales reps. Eventually, the company disbanded, and he moved to the oil and gas industry, where his success continued.

One thing I noticed that was consistent about our top-producing reps was their attitude. They had thick skin and refused to buy into negative thoughts and behavior. Josh was the leader of the pack.

Years passed, and Josh and I reunited in the business world. True to his nature, Josh is even more positive, compassionate, and driven than before. So, when he asked me to write his foreword for this fantastic book, I was honored and humbled. (Humble is not a word that typically describes me, either.)

We need more people like Josh. To be like him, we must always fill ourselves with encouraging and nutritious thoughts. Many of us do this with conditioning and repetition by keeping books like this around, reading them over and over and over again. Inspired, like new, every time we read.

You are worthy. You deserve only the best. It is your destiny to have emotional, physical, spiritual, and financial success. Stop asking why. Ask, "Why not?" You are the head. Everything you touch prospers. God's favor is being poured out upon you. You are stepping forward into abundance and have an abundance mentality.

Every day we let all kinds of things tell us how to feel and think: commercials, other people's opinions, social media, and so on. Once you take control of what you think and feel, then you are on your way to happiness and fulfillment.

And when times get rough, and they will, when you just don't "feel it" today, and you will, pick up this book and smile again. I'm confident that you will read this book over and over again. If you haven't, why not?!

–Susan Casias, 2015

Chapter 1
Raise your Hand if you Know the Answer:
An Introduction to Enthusiasm

When was the last time you were unabashedly excited?
Was it at your current job, maybe a seminar you
attended, a vacation you took? For many of us, it may be
as far back as grade school! Do you remember
elementary school? Your teacher would ask a question
that you just knew the answer to? Your hand would
shoot up in the air with as much energy as you could

muster. Your enthusiasm ran wild! Your excitement focused fully on being chosen by the teacher. You shouted "Pick me!" or "Here, here!" and you stretched your hand as high as possible, almost lifting out of your seat with an all encompassing physical and emotional energy.

We all remember these moments of excitement. No fear or complacency, just pure unadulterated enthusiasm. How great it felt to not over think the situation, not weighing the options. We instinctively reacted with happy, energetic action. What happened to that kid? He wasn't timid. He had so much excitement pumping through his system that it was barely controllable! Where did his passion and energy go? As many of us grow older, this fire begins to dwindle. We become more reserved, and we withhold our excitement. We worry what others will think, worry about failing, and we worry about wasting our energy and enthusiasm.

Wouldn't it be great if we could revisit those childhood days, where enthusiasm could run free, without the hindrance of our fears and preconceptions?

What if there was a way to re-harness this pure enthusiasm and apply it to our daily lives? What if you could unleash your excitement and use it to build relationships, strengthen your personal convictions, gain greater acknowledgment professionally, and become truly content in your life?

You can!

You possess the ability to be genuinely enthusiastic and you can forge your way back to this childlike passion! You can nurture this unharnessed zeal for all things! For this to happen we need to know that enthusiasm is paramount!

You can take control of your life, your emotions, and the way in which you utilize your energy. No longer must you accept the complacent you, the run-of-the-mill you. You deserve more. In this book, we are going to teach you to demand better and become an Enthusiastic You!

Enthusiasm is a very powerful force. It can seem enigmatic, but once enthusiasm is harnessed it becomes fundamental to your success in all facets of your life, both personally and professionally. Enthusiasm can grant you the ability to incite passion in others. It can allow you to gain loyalty from those around you and to emphasize the right message with enough energy to make your enthusiasm unforgettable.

Today is the age of too much information, and because of this, we can no longer rely heavily on facts and data alone. People need more. They need a reason to take action. To be truly compelled, they need a message that's brimming with enthusiasm.

Of course, mustering this sort of energy is not easy. Along your journey to enthusiasm, there are many obstacles you will have to overcome. Nevertheless, you need enthusiasm to truly reach people.

Everyone wants a reason to be excited! Nobody dislikes being passionate. Genuine enthusiasm is a great feeling. It's a positive anticipation that begs to be unleashed upon the world. The problem is, too many of us feel that showing enthusiasm is somehow inappropriate. Sometimes, there's a guilt that's attached to being too excited or an embarrassment of appearing wholly happy. That sort of association is not healthy!

Many times in my life I have felt as if my enthusiasm and excitement are greater than the roles and responsibilities that I've had. It's like wearing a coat that's too small. If you ever had to suppress your excitement, you know this feeling. We need to remove the constraints and embrace the freedom behind energy and excitement. In this book, I will try to shed some light on methods I've used for overcoming mediocrity and for forging a path towards the extraordinary. My method of choice, of course, is enthusiasm. We all desire to be exceptional, but do you have the emotional strength? The psychological fortitude? The available energy reserves that will inevitably be needed?

I will tell you right now, not only do you possess these traits, you have been suppressing them for years, and they are yearning to be set free. My goal is to grab you by the collar and rescue you from the sinking despair of mediocrity by providing you with the tools to become excited again. Who knows, you just might thank me for it.

Great things await us all. Of this I have no doubt, but we won't get there by being lazy or complacent. It's going to take effort; it's going to take energy, and most of all, it's going to require enthusiasm. So from here on out, you now possess the authority, nay the responsibility, to be energetic, happy, and to wear your enthusiasm on your sleeve!

Chapter 2
Rock, Paper, Scissors, and Team Captains:
The Why and What of Enthusiasm

In today's world of laziness, apathy, and rampant lack of work ethic, enthusiasm stands out. Putting energy behind your efforts can yield better results, better relationships, and a more powerful presence.

Enthusiasm sets the tone. It allows you to set the bar and expectations higher in the form of excitement. Sometimes, you have to make people get really freaking pumped up! And the only way to do that is through

enthusiasm.

I realize that enthusiasm may not seem like an innate thing, but it comes from the drive and desire to succeed; it must be practiced, and it must be pursued. Now, when we get excited about something, people around us usually have two reactions: 1) they get excited with us (which is awesome), or 2) they think you are bit crazy, which is fine. You don't want to hang out with this second group anyway. (This is not a blanket pass for you to go act psychotic.)

When cultivated correctly, the right style of enthusiasm can inspire others into terrific efforts. Small setbacks have the opportunity to ruin your day or fuel your drive to succeed; it's your choice.

In life, you must learn to recognize those who help you call upon your own enthusiasm as well as those who suck energy from you. I call these people energy vampires. They can steal your excitement and make you feel like you're just spinning your wheels when you're actually making progress. Have you ever had a colleague who always asked for your help but took credit for the work themselves? Or have you ever had a friend who always wants to talk but never wants to listen? These types of interactions can leave you feeling drained and exhausted. Life is much too short to spend time with people who break us down. We have to seek out people who positively influence our attitudes and energy levels. We also need to strive to be this sort of positive influence on others.

We have to make it a priority to fly with the eagles and starve the turkeys. We all know the turkeys; they're the people who say "You can't do that," or "You're too excitable." They try to calm us down; they distract us from our goals. The end result of their efforts is that we become a turkey. We end up just running around squawking with no direction. Turkeys are great at creating lots of noise but making no progress. What we need to do is look towards the eagles, the influencers in our lives who get things done, the people who always seem to have a greater calling and a drive to succeed. That's why we must fly with eagles and starve the turkeys. Don't give the naysayers time they don't deserve. Instead, focus on the positive. Set your sights on higher aspirations. Be one with the eagles and don't degrade yourself to the boundaries of the common riffraff. When I was a child, my friend's mother used to tell us "You can't fly with the eagles if you are hanging out with the turkeys." This was a subtle suggestion to be wary about whom we decided to hang out, but it can be applied to so many other things and still has a lot of bearing in adulthood. If we hang around with pessimistic people, we can easily become just as negative.

Who we choose to spend time with has a huge effect on who we are as a person, how we act, how we speak, and even on how well we perform in our careers. We have to be careful about who we let influence us, whether directly or indirectly.

There is statistical research that indicates that people will earn within 15% of the average income of the eight people they spend the most time with.

If who we hang around can have such an influence on our income, their influence on our attitude must be just as impactful. Maybe even more so!

We all have that one friend who approaches everything in life with a woe is me attitude. To them, everything is a struggle or a hassle. Their lives are like a sad country song. This type of attitude is detrimental. What is this person really providing to the world around them? At most they just make people around them feel a little bit better about their own lives, but mostly they bring others down to their level to wallow in a sea of self-pity. These types of people often find it hard to be happy for you and your successes as well. Heaven forbid you share some good news with them. For our own well-being we need to avoid these types of people! Negative thinking is contagious and it spreads very easily.

Remember when you were a kid and teams were being picked before playing a game or sport? Instinctively, the two oldest or tallest kids would step forward to be the team captains. After a paper, rock, scissors style decision, the winner would make the first pick of his teammates. Did all the kids just stand there looking at the ground? Did they act indifferent towards the activity? Of course not! We would smile broadly, stand up straight, puff up our chests, and even yell "Pick me!"

We all knew what they were looking for. The team captains were looking for the kids who were ready, the ones who were enthusiastic. The shy kid looking at dandelions and kicking dirt around it was never first to be chosen. He assumed he was going to be picked last, so he put no effort into looking excited. It became a self-fulfilling prophecy. If he had changed his attitude, it's very likely that he would have been chosen much sooner. He didn't seem like he wanted to be there. He lacked enthusiasm. Have you ever played the role of the dandelion kid?

In the business world, no one is ever hired because they are considered lazy, apathetic, or complacent. To succeed, what you need is great energy, presence, and a true desire to prevail. These qualities will outshine abilities any day. I was once brought into a company by a person who told me they would ". . . much rather hire someone with energy and enthusiasm than somebody with the right skill sets. Skills can be taught but it's impossible to train somebody to become energetic and enthusiastic."

Now, I agree that technical skills can be taught much easier than teaching someone to be naturally enthusiastic, but it's not impossible to train yourself to have passion and vigor behind your convictions. The key is to be committed to all your efforts, to genuinely believe in the cause you are promoting.

Everyone has been excited and enthusiastic at some point in their lives. Many times people hold themselves back from showing their full excitement for fear of being judged or ridiculed. Stop being a scaredy cat! Get out there and get excited! Get wild! By all means necessary, get enthusiastic. There's little excuse for not showing enthusiasm when you are genuinely excited, no matter your personality or surroundings.

So let's ask the question: What is enthusiasm? Can you define it? It is not always easy to define words with which we already have deep-seated impressions. When asked to identify enthusiasm, it is easy to picture someone who has energy and passion. Tigger from Winnie the Pooh comes to mind. He comes bounding into every scene bouncing around and telling others how fantastic life is! He was always happy and enthusiastic, dead set on getting others to join in his excitement. It's effortless to think of the personification of enthusiasm, but can you really explain the true essence of being enthusiastic?

Many would argue that enthusiasm means different things to different people. While this is true, I believe that the vast majority of people, when assessing the same individuals, would identify the exact same people as enthusiastic from a sample group.

What if we had to define it? Well, Webster's dictionary defines it like this -

> **en·thu·si·asm**: in'TH(y)ooze azem,
> en'TH(y)ooze azem
>
noun
> 1. feeling or showing strong excitement about
something

As concise as that is, I do not feel that it encompasses my personal affiliation with the word. It seems lacking in emotion. It doesn't capture the gut force behind it. In fact, the dictionary definition seems to cheapen the true meaning of the word.

So what words incite the correct and applicable emotions?

I would argue that passion, fervor, energy, conviction, and self-assuredness speak more truth than just "showing strong excitement."

Excitement is necessary, and energy is required, but do you have to truly believe in a cause to be enthusiastic about it?

YES.

On the surface, enthusiasm is a combination of energy and positive thinking. When you begin digging into it though, you will see it is much deeper and much more all-encompassing than you ever imagined.

Enthusiasm inspires! Enthusiasm invests! Enthusiasm excites! Enthusiasm infects, goes viral, converts, adapts, and overwhelms! Enthusiasm sells! Enthusiasm buys! And enthusiasm can inspire people to do all these things! So at this point you may think that the exclamation point on my keyboard is stuck. It's not; I'm just making a statement about using emphasis to emote excitement. I want you to get excited about being excited.
When you are truly enthusiastic, success will come more easily, happiness will be less fleeting, and your relationships will be more genuine!

In this book, we will try and show you how enthusiasm can overcome adversity and how it can be harnessed to project, promote, and inspire. Enthusiasm is a very powerful tool and should be recognized as such. Though it is necessary in our daily efforts, it is precious in its application. We are all called to show enthusiasm, but few of us accept this call. We must also understand the value and the responsibility of inciting passion in others. This is not a method for manipulation or a rationalization. Enthusiasm must be deeply intertwined with our own personal beliefs. We must understand the impact our excitement has and be prepared to lead the people who follow us because of this passion.

We must have enthusiasm, but we mustn't neglect its origin. It comes from within.

Exercises:

- When was the last time you played the role of the unenthusiastic dandelion kid?

- How could you have changed your attitude or the attitude of those around you?

- Name one person in your life who motivates you and can get you excited? I challenge you to speak with this person daily for one week and see how you feel at the end of it.

Chapter 3
Roller Coasters, Sharks, and Middle School Dances:

Overcoming Adversity when Facing Fear, Doubt, and the Common Naysayer

The only use of an obstacle is to be overcome. All that an obstacle does with brave men/women is not to frighten them, but to challenge them. –Woodrow Wilson

How can I be fearless?

Well, you can't. Fear is an obstacle that everyone has to overcome, but not everyone overcomes fear in the same way.

Fear can paralyze the most self-assured, enthusiastic person. It can infect the capable and confident with doubt and worry. No matter who you are, you must overcome fear at some time or another. When preparing a presentation for senior management, heading into a performance review, or preparing to skydive, fear can dampen our spirits, diminish our enthusiasm, and make us less of the person we truly are.

Can you overcome fear? Of course. There are many techniques out there to help you courageously stand your ground.

> *Courage is not the absence of fear, but*
> *rather the judgment that something else*
> *is more important than fear.*
> *–Ambrose Redmoon*

You have to turn the tables on your doubt! Force your fear to justify itself. Does it even deserve to be there? Fear and doubt are constantly there in the shadows, waiting for that moment when your resolve weakens. Doubt doesn't take vacations. It doesn't rest when you've had a long day. This is what makes it so easy to lose our passion. Fear and doubt hitch a ride with their good friends, tired and lazy.

It is always when we are most tired that self-doubt and worry strike the hardest. It can be very easy to give in to the path of least resistance and become a spectator in our own lives. We lose sight of the reasons we were enthusiastic in the first place.

Can you recall a time when your fear overwhelmed the initial excitement you had?

When I was a child, we used to visit an amusement park every year. As I grew older, I began looking forward to the day I would be tall enough to ride the really big roller coasters. I remember heading to the park one fateful day, knowing that the time had come. I was finally tall enough to join the big kids on larger rides. I was practically running through the parking lot. We purchased our tickets and headed into the park. I chose to head directly to the largest, most rickety, wooden roller coaster they had. I was still beaming with anticipation. I neared the entrance to the line and stood next to the "Must be this tall to ride" sign. Sure enough, I was tall enough! As we waited in the switch backed line we could see the riders on the coaster. I could hear the creaking of track as the cars zoomed by. Also audible were the screams of fear and elation coming from the riders. It was at this point that I began to worry. I began to doubt that I should be there. I wondered if I should have waited until next year and should get out of line.

I had totally lost the excitement that had overwhelmed me through the morning. I was only focusing on my fear instead of remembering why I was so happy and enthusiastic before. Luckily, my fear of embarrassment for getting out of line outweighed my fear of the roller coaster. I stayed in line and thoroughly enjoyed the ride. Afterwards, I proudly got back in line for another ride. What had I been so afraid of? Why was I so worried about this new experience?

We've all felt the impending fear that comes from the unknown. Fear and worry are terrible feelings. In most cases, our worst fears almost never come to fruition, and many times they have no bearing in reality!

Another great example of this comes from my childhood summers. I used to go swimming at the neighborhood pool. It was a large pool and was always buzzing with activity. Even though I frequented this pool often, I had a very unrealistic fear. Believe it or not, I feared that there were sharks in the deep end of the pool. Whenever I would jump off the diving board, as soon as I hit the water I would make a mad dash for the side of the pool. As ridiculous as it sounds, in my mind I could picture the shark swimming after me as I headed for the ladder. Mentally, I could see his teeth snapping shut right as I pulled my leg from the water, barely escaping. Needless to say, my childlike imagination was quite active. However, this has become a perfect metaphor for many of our common fears. Can you think of a time when you let fear get the best of you? It is very easy for our minds to manifest terrible scenarios that in most cases are very unlikely or even impossible. It's very important that we keep our imaginations at bay so that we don't let our fear overwhelm our excitement. Don't worry about sharks in the pool!

Many people waste precious moments worrying before exciting events. Assume that someone is about to give a very important speech or presentation; in this sort of scenario they would worry about the possible mistakes, about eye contact, or whether this is their target audience. In reality, worrying at this stage is truly a wasted emotion. Worry should be sorted out well before you head to the podium. This is why people practice speeches. Practicing allows us to consider all possible issues ahead of time and to mentally prepare for these events.

Another great example is when people begin to worry about the what-ifs. What if our plane crashes? What if I pass out on mile 15 of the marathon I'm going to run? What if our raft flips in the rapids? What if, what if, what if. . . .

Considering the possible scenarios is understandable and

is a phase in planning, but worrying about the outcomes to the point where it affects your ability to perform is when fear begins to run rampant. Having a bit of concern is quite healthy and can keep you on your toes, but allowing fear to force you into inaction is a terrible thing.

What people need to realize is that these moments that can cause great anxiety should actually be relished! These are opportunities to shine, to be your best, to show the world your conviction, and to share your excitement.

The greatest weapon against fear and doubt is confidence, which we will cover in the next chapter. Fear, whether real or imagined, has the ability to sabotage opportunities in our lives.

When thinking about fear, I often think of one specific event in my adolescence; I was 12 years old and still very awkward, especially around the opposite sex. There was a school-sponsored dance, and my friends and I were not going to miss it. For the days leading up to the event, I practiced dancing. I wanted to step on the floor and have a circle of people surround me, cheering me on. I practiced in the mirror making sure I had my style just right. When the day finally arrived, I was more than ready. I had all the confidence a 12-year-old boy could muster. I was going to be the cool kid with all the moves. I would woo the cutest girls and be the talk of my school for months to come.

Now, between us, I am a horrible dancer. Just awful. But the confidence I had manifested told me the exact opposite.

I remember walking into the dance; the music playing, the lights blinking. If I told you that my confidence was still intact I would be lying. I was scared for my life. All the hope and excitement came crumbling down upon me. I feared all the fears a middle schooler could fear. I feared I would get laughed at or that I'd fall down in front of everyone. The thought of ripping my pants in full view of the entire 8th grade crossed my mind more than once. At this point, I wish I could tell you that I overcame my fear, that I stepped out onto the dance floor and strutted around while the other guys in my grade were jealous. Unfortunately, that is not how things went.

I had no idea where the confident, smirking, head nodding person from my mirror went. I slinked to the side of the gym and watched. I tried to act cool and aloof, but deep down I knew I had succumbed to my own fear. My confidence had been shattered by reality. My fear of failure and judgment had overtaken my

enthusiasm.

However, that night I saw something amazing. It is the only other vivid memory I have from this dance. I watched as another kid in my grade, unpopular and nondescript, went to the center of the dance floor and summoned the courage that I did not have. I remember thinking "How is he so cool? How can he not care what he looks like to everyone else here? How is he not afraid of being ridiculed?"

Truth be known, he was not a very good dancer either, but somehow everyone rallied around his efforts. People weren't drawn to his dancing skills, they were drawn to the confidence he had while doing it. It was a confidence that was unapologetic. The self-assuredness to throw caution and nervousness to the wind and just own it.

Something that became very evident to me that evening is that confidence can be the key to pleasing a crowd, even when you lack the skills or talent.

What is important to realize is that fear doesn't have to be crippling. It doesn't have to be hiding in the shadows. It's really best just to bring it out into the light, to admit it exists. You have to point it out and declare that you know it's there! If you recognize that fear is inevitable and it will have to be overcome sooner or later, then you are way ahead of the game.

Deciding that the end goal is more important than the fear you have is a huge step towards self-confidence. We have to remember that fear lives within ourselves. It is manifested internally and grows deep within, until it overwhelms us so much that it spills out and is displayed physically. This worry, this self-doubt is yours to control. It is yours to conquer.

There are many techniques for overcoming fear. There are support groups, brain exercises, and even mental tricks that can often mask the most blatant signs of fear. It's up to each of us to understand what tactics work best for us and to use them.

Motivational speaker Tony Robbins has developed an interesting way of helping people with fear. During his seminars he often has people walk across hot coals! Truly burning coals. People are not injured during these feats of mind over matter, but it is much deeper than just no longer fearing burning your feet. It's actually more than metaphoric and can affect us psychologically. What Mr. Robbins is providing is something that can be applied to many other facets of our lives. These demonstrations help retrain our minds to question fear. Once we begin questioning fear, it loses much of the power it has over us. All of a sudden, our minds begin to think "If my fear of the hot coals was arbitrary, what other fears have I been harboring needlessly?"

I too have a technique that I use for overcoming my fear. It's quite simple by comparison, because who can take burning coals with them everywhere they travel?
What I do is a simple mind exercise. First, I identify the fear. It may not always have a specific name, but I consciously recognize its existence. Then I play through the worst possible outcomes in my head. I ask myself, what is the worst case scenario? The most terrible outcome?

Once that is identified, I ask myself a single question: could I handle it?

Of course I can! No matter what, on the other side of what I am trying to accomplish, things will be ok. Even if we do fail, we are provided with an opportunity to learn. People talk about failing forward, where we use our mistakes to propel us towards our goal. These are opportunities to learn. We must not shy away from fear, because if we do, we are then much less likely to take risks that could lead to success.

No risk, no reward.
If we don't learn from our mistakes we are doomed to repeat them.
We fall so we can learn to get back up.

What are phrases like this trying to tell us? Why are they so commonly referenced? It's because success is always preceded by failures and/or lessons.

Thomas Edison created thousands of prototypes before he came up with a working incandescent light bulb. He did not claim that he failed; he famously said that he learned 10,000 ways to not make a light bulb.
Failures are actually just ways to learn, adjust, and focus our efforts. We can't let the fear of failure hold us back.

We get to decide whether a failure makes us a better person or a bitter person. We can only progress by breaking through our discouraged paradigms and adjusting our aim.

*Losers quit when they fail. Winners fail
until they succeed.
–Robert Kiyosaki*

Adversity should not be something to fear but something to anticipate and appreciate. It's the opportunity to learn and to overcome. It can strengthen your position and allow you to better navigate issues in the future.

By anticipating possible outcomes and understanding that failure is not perpetual, it is easy to develop a higher sense of self-realization. Once you have thought through the possible outcomes, following through in the face of fear is a lot easier.

Though there are many ways to overcome issues, it is important to remember that fear and negativity can seep deep into our emotional well-being. They have the power to change how we think and how we react and can even affect our relationships and our careers. People will treat someone differently if they seem skittish or worried.

When I was younger, I hung out frequently with a with a group of friends. One friend in particular, we'll call him Bob, used to always talk about his latest setback. Many times, Bob's trials and tribulations were mildly entertaining. He would share his latest story about his car getting towed, losing his wallet, or getting broken up with by his girlfriend. It seemed like nothing good ever happened to Bob. He saw all these things as though the world was out to get him. Over time, Bob's pessimistic outlook began to bring everyone around him down. We all stopped finding his attitude amusing and saw Bob as depressing. Slowly, we stopped inviting him to join us and we lost touch. Nobody wanted this perpetual party pooper to ruin our good time. Bob's negative attitude made things worse for himself. He lost touch with several friends and he most likely did not realize his pessimism was the cause.

How likely are you to invite someone to lunch who is perpetually pessimistic?

Doom and gloom do not forge healthy relationships, and they certainly do not help in social or professional settings. For our own well-being, as well as those around us, it is important to strive towards a positive outlook. Negativity is not going to improve your circumstances.

Negative thinking is a product of fear and anxiety. Just because you are afraid does not mean you have to accept the worst. Fear does have the ability to cripple people into failure and inaction, but it also has the ability to motivate individuals to be their best and operate at the peak of their abilities.

It is up to you to develop the best method to personally combat and overcome fear.

> *The only thing we have to fear, is fear*
> *itself. –FDR*

President Roosevelt had it right. It's all in our heads. We all have fear and we all must overcome it.

How you view and handle fear is up to you, but I believe that one of the best antidotes for fear is confidence.

Exercises:

- When have you let fear dampen your excitement and prevent you from doing something?

- How do you wish this scenario had gone differently?

- What are three things someone could have said to you then that would have alleviated your fear? Say those things to yourself right now, out loud.

Chapter 4
Tricycles and Red Wagons:
Prepare for Frustration

When you're a very ambitious person,
the things that are disappointing are
when other people around you aren't as
enthusiastic. –Reba McEntire

Have you ever had a problem getting other people excited? Can you think of a time you tried to rally the troops only to be shut down? Have you ever been in charge of a group project at work or school with team members that were apathetic? This chapter explores how great enthusiasm can sometimes bring great frustration. Anyone who has fought to share their passion only to be silenced or rejected knows this feeling.

You can put forth your best effort, and things can still go wrong. Even with the greatest intentions and plans things can just fall apart, but that's ok.

We cannot blame ourselves in these sorts of situations, and we cannot allow ourselves to be afraid of them. We should not allow setbacks to dampen our spirits or our enthusiasm. It is important that we strive to maintain our intensity and passion when faced with this adversity.

You still deserve the proverbial gold star for effort.

Please note that this is not a blanket excuse to neglect details, but we all know that sometimes our hard work can feel like it was done in vain. These things can become very mentally taxing and it can easily take hold of our emotional well-being.

Even minor setbacks can create huge amounts of frustration. If you are truly enthusiastic about something, you are bound to face frustration. You have to rise above these issues and double your efforts. Overcoming these types of setbacks can reinvigorate your excitement and solidify your resolve. In the end, we have to bounce back and march forth once again.

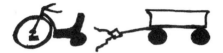

Frustration is common when faced with trials and tribulations at any age. When I was four years old, I decided that I wanted to attach my red, radio flyer wagon to the back of my tricycle and excitedly set about accomplishing this task. Using an old coat hanger, I looped the bent ends through the wagon's handle and around the seat post of the trike. After the wagon was attached, I climbed on the tricycle and begin to pedal. As I began to move forward the wagon broke free. Undeterred, I backed up the tricycle and reattach it, but once again the trike separated from the wagon. I tried again without success. I had images running through my head of me riding proudly up and down the street with the wagon in tow; I was not going to be defeated this easily. I kept trying. This happened seven or eight times and then finally, I broke down from frustration. The disappointment was overwhelming. Tears welled up in my eyes. My excitement had all but vanished. My frustration had bled into anger and eventually sadness. It was a very bad day for the four-year-old me.

If you are wondering how a four-year-old could retain such vivid memories, he didn't. This little ordeal was captured on film by my parents, which begs more questions that probably shouldn't be answered. Nevertheless, frustration has a way of growing and building until it's much larger than the problem that caused it. If unchecked, small inconveniences can become very overwhelming. Just like the four-year-old boy sitting there trying to attach a wagon to his trike, we all need to keep things in perspective.

Frustration happens just as easily in the business world. I was working in sales for a medium sized software company. Our business was steady, but our leadership team was always looking for ways to expand our customer base and increase our efficiency. One of the larger problems was our disorganized, inefficient work-flow for how sales orders were processed. When they were a smaller company, it made sense to have an agile, adaptable process, but as the company grew it became apparent that staged work-flows were desperately needed. When client orders would come in, important things like contacts and maintenance schedules would be missing. The process for getting our software in the hands of the client was foggy and convoluted. Things would get lost in the cracks.

The management recognized that the company needed to formalize the process. They explored options that would take the administrative work out of the hands of the sales people so their time was free to pursue interactions with clients. This was a great idea! The entire sales team was very excited and supportive. It would allow us to focus on our core business and streamline the process from order to delivery. More time selling, less time pushing paper! This was going to be a huge help, or so we thought.

We held a kick-off round table discussion and several planning and implementation meetings. After a lot of preparation, we began using the new process. It consisted of stage gates for each step in the sales process. Once the salesperson filled out all the correct information they would submit it and the process would take over. Then a series of managers, lawyers, and contracts people would get to approve their respective piece. It seemed to be working like a charm, until I received a call from an irate client. Their software access had been shut off! It turns out they had never received their permanent licenses. As I began investigating, their order was still held up in one of our departments. The person with the authority to approve this step was on vacation. This particular sale was at a standstill.

As a team, we had been so excited about getting the menial paperwork issues off our plates that we never saw the huge bottleneck in the process. While it took less handholding by the sales people, the time from sale to delivery had actually lengthened. The frustration was felt by everyone involved. We no longer had the flexibility or the discretion to move things through the process. With single points of failure, we often had to circumvent the stages by getting management involved. It was cumbersome to say the least. In fact it became a larger hindrance to our business than the original disorganization. Something we had been so gung-ho about became a huge source of frustration. Eventually the entire process was scrapped.

Whether it is in a business environment or in our personal lives, frustrations are bound to happen. Things rarely pan out exactly as we want them to, but that's no reason to be reserved in our enthusiasm. We can't be guarded in our excitement, even if we have prior experiences with disappointment and frustration. We have to look at every situation as an opportunity to be excited.

When I am faced with setbacks, I use several methods to

help overcome them. One of the best methods I've used is to consciously take time to reflect and choose to be decisive. By doing this you can help to overcome minor hindrances. Reflection gives you a moment to evaluate your position and to confirm or denounce that the obstacle is legitimate. Too often, people do not take enough time to let the initial shock of a setback die down. They move to decision too quickly. If you give yourself enough of a pause before making decisions and taking action, you will find that many of the things that we worry about work themselves out. Reflection gives you the opportunity to reset your goals and your expectations. It's more than coming to terms with a situation; it's an effort in coming to conclusions and eventually identifying solutions.

Next, you have to make the decision to be decisive. It's important that we add a time frame on this. Otherwise, people spend too much time reflecting and can succumb to analysis paralysis. We have to take action, and we have to do it deliberately. Taking the time to understand a situation and make a finite decision is important.

When you truly ponder a situation, true priorities can become clearer, options seem more plentiful, and often the problem itself can begin to look menial.

However, it is important to know that contemplation is great as long as a timely decision is reached. Many times, more is lost by indecision than wrong decision.

Another method that is infinitely helpful is perspective. This little gem can save days, weeks, or even months of heartache and turmoil. Getting someone else's opinion on a situation often gives us a much-needed 10,000 ft. view. Many times, we are too close to a problem to see the simple solutions. When we are stuck in the swamp, fighting our way ahead, it can be easy to miss the paved road that is right next to us.

Perspective gives you the invaluable chance to see through someone else's eyes. When searching out insight of this nature, who you choose to speak with is very important.

Often, we seek out people who would sympathize and be a shoulder to cry on. They are not the people to give you perspective. If you seek out someone for sympathy, it is too easy for you to play the victim. What you need is someone who will be brutally honest and objective. Now, I'm not suggesting that you corral a stranger at the local Starbucks to plea your sob story, but it does help if the person is a bit removed from the situation. We need to hear the reality of our problem. We need to hear the truth.

That's where mentors can be very helpful.

With perspective from the right mentor, we can more easily identify ways to overcome our adversities. Sometimes we can even realize that our roadblocks were artificially manifested in our heads. Perspective is a fantastic tool for facing fear, overcoming obstacles, and dealing with frustration.

We can be frustrated by so many things in our lives: our jobs, our families, traffic, politics, etc. Anything can become the epicenter for frustration. All it takes is a small amount to bleed into other areas of our lives.

Like most things in our lives, we have a lot more control over it than we admit. It's all in your attitude! Most likely you don't want to carry the burden of frustration, and you don't have to. You have the power to let things go and make the conscious decision to move on.

Exercises:

- Think of a time when it was difficult to excite those around you. Were these people affected by the outcome of their inaction?

- List three daily frustrations you face. How could you mitigate the impact these have on your attitude?

- Choose one frustration you have and make a conscious decision to not let it bother you anymore.

Chapter 5
Lightning and Fly Balls:
People Respect Confidence

When you have confidence, you can
have a lot of fun. And when you have a
lot of fun, you can do amazing things.
–Joe Namath

For most people, confidence seems to come in small
spurts. Over time, things begin build up and then get
pushed out in the form of self-assuredness. Eventually,

these feelings fade and we go back to quiet complacency. For many, confidence only comes in small doses, during fleeting moments of glory. These moments are so rare and special that we pine over them when they are gone. It's like watching lightning, where it appears suddenly and illuminates everything for a brief moment, and then it's gone. We yearn for more opportunities to feel that internal self-assurance, to be brimming with confidence. We want to have the true landscape revealed!

What I suggest to people is to not allow confidence to be so rare. I would argue that we all have reasons to be confident in our abilities and our actions. We need to take great efforts to understand that confidence is not about being arrogant, it's about being justifiably assured in your abilities. It's about feeling happy about being you!

We don't want confidence to only show up in extreme

moments. We need confidence to be a continual passenger on our journey. Being self-assured can give us encouragement to try new things and inspiration to believe that we can accomplish anything we set our minds to.

It may seem minor, but I'm referring to the kind of confidence you have when you get the perfect haircut, when you give a fantastic presentation to your boss, or when you get a huge compliment from somebody you respect. I'm talking about the confidence you get from exceeding people's expectations and being praised for hard work.

In my youth, I played little league baseball every year. Truth be told, I was far from a star player. I was relegated to a spot late in the batting order and I only played positions in the outfield. As excited as I always was to be part of the team, I was never the one who was hitting home runs or making big plays. One game, I was standing in center-field, trying my best to pay attention to the game—little league outfielders do not see nearly as much action as players near the bases. My hat was adjusted just right, I punched my mitt with my fist a few times for good measure, and then I patiently waited for some action. Suddenly, there was a crack! Everyone's eyes shot towards the sky. The other team had just got a huge hit and it was headed right for center-field. After a couple of shuffled steps, I shoved my glove into the air. I had lost sight of the ball and was hoping for the best, and then I heard a loud slap as the ball landed directly in my glove! Cheers came from the stands! I was elated! As I walked back the dugout, I was grinning ear to ear. So proud and excited, the smile never left my face for the duration of the game. That night, my coach gave me the coveted game ball. This was reserved for the player who contributed the most to the game. I walked away from the field that night feeling a foot taller than I actually was. The confidence I gained from that one moment led me to work harder at practices and to pay even more attention during the games. Now that I *knew* that I could accomplish great things, I set about looking for opportunities to do just that.

It's not necessarily these specific moments that we need to recreate, but it's the internal emotions that go with them. The moments that make you stand up taller and grin a little wider. We are provided with a sneak peek of how we should approach life. We cannot be timid; we need to expect the opportunity to accomplish greatness! We need more times in our lives where we don't just *think* we can take on the world but when we *know* that we can!

> *All you need in this life is ignorance and*
> *confidence, and then success is assured.*
> *–Mark Twain*

Whether Mark Twain was being sarcastic or not, it doesn't change that fact that confidence is a very powerful tool. I am not going to lie: harnessing confidence daily is not easy. It would be practically impossible to expect anyone to be able to maintain it perpetually. However, it can become a more natural disposition with practice. It takes an internal peace and a mind that is not conflicted. The more at peace you are with yourself, the more self-assured you can be.

Confidence can mean the difference between a cubicle and a corner office with a view. People often wonder why seemingly less qualified or less intelligent people become successful. Many times the answer is **confidence**.

Being confident and convicted in your actions makes you more believable and more likely to gain support from those around you. Confidence can be as blatant as banging your fist on a desk and demanding that people see things from your perspective, or it can be a subtle as holding your head high, making people wonder if you know something they don't.

We all have our own ways of creating enthusiasm in ourselves. We say phrases like "You can do it," "You're the best," "You've got this," and "You're doing great." These phrases or mantras can excite, energize, and motivate us. If you don't have one, I suggest you adopt one! Whether we're channeling someone else's praise or just pumping ourselves up internally, everyone needs a little nudge of encouragement and motivation. Identify your phrase and make it part of your daily routine!

Everyone gets nervous in certain situations. However, nervousness can easily be transitioned into energy and enthusiasm. What nervousness truly represents is repressed anxiousness. Our bodies respond to anxiety and exhilaration in practically the same way: increased heart rate, intense focus, and a sense of hyper-awareness. If harnessed, nervous energy can be very useful and effective.

Instead of having these things hold us back, we should

change our thought processes to recognize anxiety and channel it into excitement and enjoyment. If we can recognize and overcome our anxieties, there are few mental limits to what we can accomplish. We need to harness our energy and transition it into confidence.

You can read motivational quotes or review other people's successes, but none of those things are a substitute for direct encouragement. When at-a-boys are directed at you, they become personal. You internalize them. You begin to truly believe what you're being told, and that is exactly what you need to do. Believe!

When you need a boost of confidence, when you're about to walk into an important meeting, when you are about to ask a cute somebody out on a date, or when you need to muster some self-assurance, what runs through your head?

I can tell you what's running through my head: rock music. Actually, it is a very cheesy 80s song: "You're the Best Around." Though this song has long since been over looked for a Grammy, its motivational quality gets me fired up every time I hear it. The song itself is not lyrically deep or even musically technical. It just makes me feel like I can take on the world, like no problem is too difficult and no issue insurmountable. I unconsciously nod my head up and down, as if to physically say "YES! Yes, I am the best around!!"

Imagine how enthusiastic you could be with the theme music from *Rocky* following you around all day. It might actually be a little much, but I'm sure you can imagine the feeling.

Channeling your energy into excitement can put you at the top of your game, and it's a great way to curb fear and nervousness.

We all have our own ways to prepare for taking on a mentally or physically taxing endeavor. I often question my methods for preparation and adjust them for the environment I am in. Do I get nervous? Of course I do, but I work hard to channel this nervousness into excitement and enthusiasm. It's a technique I use quite often. It's something that can be utilized before first dates, job interviews, important meetings, or big speeches.

Here's how I do it:

>   *Make sure you are prepared!* I cannot stress that enough. Whether it is setting up dinner reservations for a date, or researching a

company's offerings before a job interview, preparation is crucial. Preparation keeps you from looking foolish and having to backtrack. People don't get lucky, they get prepared. Planning gives you a strong foundation, which allows you to easily understand and adapt in any given scenario. Being confident is easy when you are prepared.

Know your audience! Making sure you know the type of people who will be present. When people are nervous, they can overcompensate by being curt or by acting arrogant. Don't insult people by talking down to them, and don't over-complicate your message. Remember, every person is human and they know you are too.

Don't worry about making mistakes. Everyone makes them, but few people are smart enough to not highlight them. It's ok to mess up! If you err during a speech or discussion, feel free to acknowledge it and move on. Make light of your misstep if possible. Just don't focus on it. Revisiting a mistake will only solidify it in the minds your listeners.

Have fun! People enjoy a bit of levity. They like being able to relate and enjoy someone else's comments. Being friendly and personable will give you a lot of leeway with any mistakes or errors. People do not connect because of someone's sterile demeanor. No one ever walked away from a business presentation and praised it for being very serious. No one ever says "I like them. They seem stern!" Be happy. Have fun.

Use the back pocket theory. Now, this is my best secret for overcoming fear. I know that no matter how this conversation or presentation goes, I have something bigger and better in my back pocket. I know that this meeting, interview, or speech may be important, but it is not the most important thing to me. I psych myself into thinking "I am going to do my best and that the people listening can take it or leave it." Their approval does not make me a better or worse person. I keep this special confidence in my back pocket. It's better to fail in a spectacular manner than not to have tried at all.

Disclaimer: Channeling nervousness into positive energy is a valuable way to focus and progress. However, I would caution people when channeling too much nervousness; the excitement can get a bit out of hand. In fact, I've been known to speak too quickly during speeches. One time I was invited to give a half hour talk to a group of 200 data managers. I know what you're thinking, data managers are the first thing that comes to mind with regards to enthusiasm. Right. I was slated for 30 minutes, and using my technique, I wasn't nervous, but I was really excited. I had practiced for weeks before, adding lots of humor and lightheartedness, and always ending with just enough time for questions. About 26 minutes. When the time arrived, I took the stage and presented to the crowd. I enjoyed it and felt like I reached my audience. I concluded my talk, and as the people where applauding I looked at my watch. On this day, I finished my speech in just over 14 minutes. Half the time allotted! I was mortified. Then, remembering my method, I decided that some humor was needed. I joked that I do not take questions. Everyone laughed, and my presentation ended on a high note. Luckily, the timing had little bearing on the message I had given.

To my relief, people were commending me on the humor I used and on the enthusiasm that I had for the topic of data management. No one noticed they had an extra 15 minutes for a coffee and bathroom break.

With this knowledge, I often have to force myself to slow down. As I slow down, I can periodically take stock of how things are going and adjust accordingly. Rhythm and cadence are important when channeling anxious energy into enthusiasm. Generally, your enthusiasm is just as important as what you are saying; however, this controlled excitement needs to be practiced and exercised.

Keep this in mind as you transition your mind from one that's nervous to one that is excited.

The moral here is to be enthusiastic, but make sure you stay focused. Be deliberate with your energy.

I do not want to harp on this point, but it must be acknowledged: confidence is a positive trait; it should never be associated with arrogance or bigotry. Self-deprecation is just as bad. It is never enjoyable to be around someone who seeks to be pitiful or arrogant. I try my best to avoid both.

Confidence, on the other hand, is great.

In most cases, showing genuine enthusiasm can be just as convincing as facts and supporting data. People like to join in other people's excitement, to be part of that energy, and they love a reason to become excited. Can you give them that reason?

Exercises:

- When was the last time you consciously pumped yourself up?

- What was the method you used for getting excited?

- What is your confidence-boosting mantra or phrase? I challenge you to say it out loud to yourself every day for one week.

- How has this impacted your self perception?

Chapter 6
Mt. Everest vs. the Realists:
A Look into Being Optimistic

I believe that success in life is made by
going into an area with blind, furious
optimism.
–Sylvester Stallone

Being enthusiastic is a lot of work, but most of the time
it is rewarded many times over. A vital part of
enthusiasm is a positive attitude. No one ever motivated
others into greatness by sharing a pessimistic attitude.
Optimism is essential for being enthusiastic.

We all know that hard work often yields the best results. It is the same with enthusiasm. If you work at being energetic and positive, then the results will be paid back in huge returns. What's great about enthusiasm is that the more you practice it, the easier it becomes to naturally have it. Eventually, you will become an energetic, naturally enthusiastic person without having to put in as much effort.

The hard work of striving to be passionate and positive retrains your attitude and your mindset. We have all heard that it's good to think positively, but what if you could train yourself to be optimistic?

You can. It just takes hard work and initiative.

> *The only time success comes before work is in the dictionary.*
> *–Vidal Sassoon*

Optimism has different meanings to different people. To me, it is purely about a positive attitude. To others, optimists are unrealistic and sometimes even simple-minded people. There is a misconception that optimistic people don't know enough to be cautious and they don't always live in the real world.

This sort of attitude is defeatist, and it's detrimental to archiving your goals.

No one ever summited Mount Everest while thinking "I probably won't reach the top." No one ever received a promotion from their boss because they had a pessimistic outlook. Never in the history of mankind was it uttered "That depressed guy sure knows how to motivate everyone."

You have to *believe* that you can reach your goals! You have to desire and expect great outcomes from your efforts. Go forward with determination. Strive for greatness! Don't expect the worst! You have to think positively!

Good things happen to those that expect good things to happen. If you focus only on the negative, that's all you will see.

Optimism plays a huge role in success, whether it's looking for a parking spot in the first row or applying for your dream job. We have to be positive if we want good things to happen.

In high school, a good friend of mine had a huge crush on one of the prettiest girls in our school. She was on the track team and she was one of the school's cheerleaders. In direct opposition, my friend was a very average guy and was one of my soccer teammates.

One day we were on the practice field doing passing drills. The girl's track team was practicing as well. My friend stepped over to me and said "Do you see that girl over there? I'm going to take her to the homecoming dance." He said it in such a matter of fact manner that I assumed she had already said yes. "You're going with her!?" I exclaimed. "When did you ask her?" He explained that he had not asked her yet, but it was just a matter of time.

The running joke on the soccer team was that she would string him along and there was no chance that they would end up together. Over the next few weeks, I watched him continually approach her during lunch or in the hallways. He always maintained a huge smile when he walked up to her, even after receiving the cold shoulder the first couple times. She was always a bit standoffish, but slowly it became apparent that she was becoming more willing to talk with him. This continued until one fateful day when I saw them holding hands.

How on earth had he done it?! He predicted it! He said he was going to take her to the homecoming dance and sure enough, they ended up going to the dance together. He believed he could take her to the dance and he set about doing just that. Confidence may have played its part in his efforts, but I think his positive attitude played a much larger role. Even in the face of ridicule from his friends and rejection from the girl he pursued, he was optimistic. He thought the best could happen and stayed positive. If he had listened to the people who told him to be realistic, he never would have succeeded. He didn't buy into negative thinking and neither should you.

Optimism doesn't mean someone lacks facts or is unintelligent. Optimistic people like to stare challenges in the face and look for ways to overcome them. Positive attitudes stand out far more than pessimistic or even realistic ones. Staying positive in bad situations can motivate others into thinking less bleakly. It's important for people to have a positive influence. Great leaders motivate and excite those around them. They focus on the positives. Negativity spreads much more quickly than positive attitudes. For this reason, it makes optimism and enthusiasm that much more important.

Problems and setbacks are going to happen, whether you are scaling a mountain or working on a group project in an office. People who harp on negatives are much less likely to progress past them. Once you have allowed one setback to affect your attitude, it opens the gates for the next problem to affect you even more. This can perpetuate the negativity until even the slightest inconveniences seem like major, show-stopping problems.

> *Obstacles are those dreadful things you*
> *see when you take your eyes off your*
> *goal.* –Henry Ford

If you start with a positive attitude and take each problem in stride, the chance of reaching your goals increases. Being optimistic does not directly oppose being realistic. It's a conscious choice to look for the good, to look past the obstacles in the way. When you focus on problems and setbacks, you take you mind off your goals. Life is going to throw curve-balls. We have to look for the positive, so be optimistic!

> *Optimism is the faith that leads to achievement. Nothing can be done without hope and confidence. –Helen Keller*

Being optimistic is more than just acting happy; it is about expecting the best to happen. It's about anticipating great things ahead. It really is about hope, a deep-seated knowledge that things are going well and will continue to get better. Optimism is not about being blissfully ignorant to realities and hardships of daily life; it's about looking at things in a positive light.

Have you ever spoken to a person who is perpetually negative, and yet they claim that they are just a "realist?" People often cloak themselves in phrases like "being realistic" or "living in reality" to mask their negative attitude. Many times, people who claim to be realists are just pessimists who refuse to admit it. If it quacks like pessimist and acts like a pessimist, then it's a pessimist. Negative attitudes are counterproductive and can infect people around them to similar disappointing attitudes. So what do you do if you're the pessimist? Decide to change! You need to empower yourself to be positive. Compliment yourself daily, read positive stories, and look for the good and not the negative. You choose what you ingest psychologically, so make sure it is positive!

I have a good friend that has a daily habit for making himself more optimistic. Every morning he looks at himself in the mirror and smiles 10 times in a row. Whether he feels like it or not, he forces himself to do this. According to him, this effort makes smiling throughout the day come more naturally. Even though many days he has to force himself to smile those 10 times, he finds himself feeling happier throughout the day. With this small morning ritual, his days are much more inspired and optimistic.

In the business world, optimism can make a huge difference as well. People with positive attitudes are identified as problem-solvers and are promoted sooner than their pessimistic colleagues.
When a small company I was working for was acquired by a huge firm, there were many different perspectives.

Some people believed that this larger company would allow for better career opportunities and options for advancement. However, there were many people that believed the acquisition would mean doom for their position and for the small company culture.

The assimilation process had its trials and tribulations, but the large company strove to make it as painless as possible. In the ensuing months, we moved into their offices and slowly merged our teams. It was right after we moved into their offices that our industry had a huge downturn. Within three months, the company's stock was worth practically a third of what it had been. It was a dark time. Negative thinking became more common, especially as talks of layoffs began to circulate. Though it was difficult to maintain an optimistic outlook, people tried to be positive. When the layoffs began, it was quite apparent that people who had not embraced the changes were first to be considered redundant. It was the people who were most vocal about the negative aspects of the acquisition that were asked to leave. In the company's opinion, why should they keep someone around if they were not committed to making the business successful? Those with positive attitudes were mostly retained. The company made every effort to find positions or make concessions, but only for those who kept their positive outlook.

When someone is optimistic, people generally want to assist them. Pessimistic attitudes do not inspire others to help. Positive attitudes, on the other hand, are enjoyable and desirable.

Have you ever noticed that your attitude can have a huge impact on all other facets of your life? It can even just be a small thing that sets it in motion. When someone cuts you off in traffic, it is easy to see it as a personal attack. Many times it can affect the rest if our day, building toward a string of bad events. Something like that happens and we begin to see everything through the lens of a victim. Our mood suffers, and our attitude degrades. Daily efforts become more of a grind. Even benign interactions with other people can take on an air of malice. This type of negative perception can run rampant and become a beast that perpetuates this mentality.

People talk about how bad things come in threes. I've personally experienced it. Something bad happens, and then a second thing. After that, we are looking for the next bad thing. We condition ourselves to keep an eye out for the next problem. This "What's next? Why me?" mentality is detrimental, and it builds a terrible momentum in our daily lives. In reality, it's all in our own minds. If we choose to be pessimistic, then we are going to see the bad in every situation. Nothing good can come from a pessimistic attitude.

As much as you want to believe it, you are not an innocent, unsuspecting victim. You've allowed yourself to become the victim. Don't allow situations or other people to affect you in this way. Be conscious of your emotions and surroundings. Don't be negative. Instead, look for the positive, and choose to be optimistic.

> *Virtually nothing is impossible in this*
> *world if you just put your mind to it and*
> *maintain a positive attitude.*
> *–Lou Holtz*

A positive and optimistic attitude can affect our lives just as deeply. When we choose to see the good in our situations, we tend to be on the lookout for other positive things. Have you ever noticed that when you are having an above average or great day, things tend to continue to get better and better?

Many times, our attitude and our outlook on life are up to us. Like John Cusack said in the movie *Say Anything*, "Why can't you just decide to be in a good mood and then be in a good mood?" Well, many times we can. It's our decision; we have to consciously choose to be in a good mood. It is up to us to be optimistic and to look at things in a positive light. We need to look for the good in every situation. We need to be positive in our attitudes and our actions.

Exercises:

- Name something good that happened to you today.

- Name something negative you experienced that led to something positive.

- List three positive things that happen to you each day for one week. Review them at the end of the week.

- Smile at yourself in the mirror 10 times every morning for a full week. (How has this impacted your attitude on a daily basis?)

Chapter 7
Vampires and Hide and Seek

Yup, vampires. They don't steal our blood; instead, they come after our energy, our time, and our enthusiasm. Most energy vampires do not even realize they have this sort of impact on others. Nevertheless, these people can take the wind out of our sails with a few words or actions.

When I originally thought about adding this chapter, I mentioned the title to a friend of mine whose response was, "Do you want a picture of my ex-wife to put next to it?" Though I laughed and I knew he wasn't serious, it made me second guess writing an entire chapter about the people who work against our enthusiasm. It made me think that maybe I was empowering them too much, giving them too much credit. The more I discussed it with my friend, I realized that the reason he was so quick to respond with a joke about energy vampires is because they are so widespread and because many people can immediately think of someone like this. In fact, right now I bet the majority of people who are reading this had someone flash into their minds who fits this category. For these reasons, I decided to keep this chapter. I don't want to spend too much time discussing these types of people, but it is important to identify them. In this way, we can lessen their impact on our enthusiasm and our attitudes. We need to make sure these people are not empowered to take our enthusiasm away.

I've broken them down into three types:

1: The sad/depressive; the pessimist
Sometimes, they carry an air of depression and can easily take you down this path of sadness and despair. Just being around people like this can bring you down from a great mood. These types are very difficult, if not impossible, to

motivate and excite. They carry the woe is me mentality and are often throw themselves pity parties. It is always important to have compassion for people in distress, but people who are perpetually playing the victim bring no benefit to those around them. Ominous and depressive environments are difficult to break away from. Avoid individuals who relish this type of atmosphere. They may not even be aware of their disposition, but it is detrimental to positive attitudes and therefore counterproductive to enthusiasm and success.

2: The jealous/envious

These people are practically malicious in their efforts. They cannot be enthusiastic or excited, so they don't want you to be. They try to knock you down from your happy status. They will ask you to calm down, or they directly attack your ideas by punching holes in them.

Sometimes these people even try to mask their jealousy behind a facade of concern. They say things like "I just want you to be realistic," or "I don't want you to get your hopes up." Their ultimate goal is to lessen your enthusiasm and positive energy. Many times, people of this persuasion can bait others into their sour attitude. They feed off the degradation of people's hopes and excitement. An example would be if someone was excited about moving into a new place, a jealous or envious energy vampire would only be focusing on the problems with the new place: "It's probably going to increase your commute a lot," "There really doesn't seem to be any good parking," or "Wow, you really want to live there?" Many of these could seem fairly conversational in their tone, but the underlying malevolent attitude can change a positive attitude into one of disappointment. Don't let people like this ruin the positive. Life is too short to give these types of attitudes any emotional energy.

3: The dominator/inept

This type of enthusiasm thief is much harder to identify. They may even have a lot of energy themselves. Often the loss of energy comes from one-upmanship and/or their effort to steal others' thunder. It is great to have other people with enthusiasm, as long as their efforts do not run counter to the goals at hand. Many times, these people do not even realize what they are doing. That itself makes recognizing them all the more important. They usurp stories in the middle of their telling, which leaves the person telling the story a bit despondent. Their excitement was high-jacked! These dominating energy vampires do not set out to diminish people's enthusiasm. They merely feel their input is more important. Sometimes, these people are self-centered or narcissistic, but most of the time they are just unaware of their malice.

Everyone needs to be cognizant of people they spend time with and the effects they have on our daily lives. Our mood and energy levels can be greatly influenced by people we interact with, especially those close to us.

Remember when you were a kid and a group of friends would get together for hide and seek? All that energy and excitement was palpable as the person that was it began counting out loud. "One Mississippi, two Mississippi, three Mississippi…" Everyone would scatter and begin clambering for the best hiding spots. The nearby spots would get taken pretty quickly, though anyone really good at the game knew to look for the hiding spots further away from the person counting. Once finding your spot, you would crouch down. Trying not to breath too loudly, you begin wondering who would be the first to get caught. You waited and listened. Then you'd hear it, an argument was erupting. Someone failed to find a hiding spot in time and began yelling complaints. "That's not fair!" "They took all the good spots!" "You counted too quickly!" As this person started to complain, you could feel the fun being sucked out of the game. This person would rather whine about being caught than continue the game. Now we had to spend several minutes discussing the issue and eventually start over. All the original excitement and enthusiasm had been siphoned from the game. Their negative attitude impacted everyone. They couldn't let others enjoy themselves unless they got their way. This selfishness is a prime example of how energy vampires threaten the happiness and excitement of those around them.

Though people around us may have the best intentions, many times they do not understand the negative impact that their attitudes and behaviors have. We have to be vigilant against their influence, and we have to be resolute in our efforts when faced with them.

These types of situations also happen in the corporate world. I've sat in meetings where a single individual would derail the entire meeting. Once, a team I was working with decided to collaborate on a common problem we were all facing. Our competition had been making huge inroads with many of our clients, and we needed to develop some innovative strategies to maintain our market share. With our management's prompt of "There are no bad ideas," we began tossing around some fairly abstract suggestions. There was one person in the meeting who chose to be very negative. They were quick to dismiss other people's ideas and were only focusing on the problem while not offering solutions. It made brainstorming a very difficult task. Once someone begins to criticize options, it forces people to put up a defensive front and become more reserved in their suggestions. This energy vampire was perpetuating their negativity and removing other people's enthusiasm.

Not surprisingly, no solution discovered or implemented

that day. However, the next meeting was much more productive because that particular energy vampire was absent

When someone only brings negativity to the table, they have no ability to contribute constructively. In fact, many times people like this hinder progress for everyone else.

On occasion, I've played the energy vampire without realizing it. I was out to dinner with a good friend of mine who had recently returned from a ski vacation. He was sharing some stories about his trip, including the great weather and conditions. In an effort to relate, I began talking about a ski trip I had taken. I started commenting on the amount of snow we had and how nice our accommodations had been. All of a sudden it struck me. I had high-jacked the conversation! My friend was trying to share his experience and I kidnapped it for the sake of my own ego! I had stolen his excitement and taken on the role of energy vampire. I should have let him continue talking. I should have let him maintain his enthusiasm.

Everyone has played the part of the energy vampire at one time or another. It can be easy to occasionally slip into this role. We need to recognize that we can have a negative affect on those around us if we do not keep ourselves in check. These types of opportunities are very common. Many times, in an effort to relate to someone, we can usurp a conversation without a second thought. We must be aware how easy it is to steal someone's enthusiasm. We have to make an effort to be conscientious.

Lately, one of the most common places we find energy vampires is on social media. The reason it is so rampant there is the anonymity of those platforms. Whether it's envious statements made on someone's Facebook page, digital bullying, or twitter wars, emotionally draining traps are out there in social media and we are wise to avoid them. The opinions and musings of strangers have too much power in our psyche. We need to be aware of how impactful the things we read, write, or hear can be. If need be, un-friend energy vampires and take away their power. Don't encourage, perpetuate, or participate in these types of behavior. Everyone should look to build up those around us, not break them down.

> *No one can make you feel inferior*
> *without your consent.*
> *–Eleanor Roosevelt*

It is impossible to rid our lives entirely of these types of people. The key is to know they exist, identify people who can drain us of our excitement, and to mitigate the impact we let them have on us. It is also important that we regulate our own attitudes and behaviors so they do not diminish the energy of those we interact with.

Exercises:

- Can you think of a time when someone close to you acted as an energy vampire?

- Is this a common occurrence in your relationship?

- When have you acted as an energy vampire?

- How can you adjust your life tomorrow to positively affect people's energy levels?

Chapter 8
Lets Go Camping:

Motivation isn't Enough

Enthusiasm needs a target, a direction, and someone to manifest it! This is not easy. Creating excitement and energy behind a cause can take a great deal of skill and effort.

Unrestrained enthusiasm can be inspiring, but it doesn't mean the effort is done without an idea of where you will end. Unrestrained does not mean directionless. Unrestrained refers to the freedom of being unencumbered, like driving a car without a governor to control your speed. I use the term to imply a sense of hope and a feeling of endless possibility. It does not mean unbridled or wild; rather, it means unhindered and hopeful.

Stephen Covey tells us to "Begin with the end in mind." This means, begin with a goal or an aspiration. The big goals help us navigate the dangerous terrain between where we are and where we are going. If we look only at the small problems and the day-to-day frustrations, we end up focusing on the distractions. We get sidetracked. Once we become sidetracked or stuck in the weeds, we lose sight of the aspiration, which often means more time spent on things that do not directly move you closer to your goal.

We must remember that it's the large goals that help you get up in the morning, and it's the small goals that help you get to sleep.

We have all heard that the joy is in the journey and not the destination. In fact, Ralph Waldo Emerson even said that "Life is a journey not a destination." As inspirational as quotes like this are, we cannot discount the importance that destinations and goals play in our lives. I personally have trouble staying focused and enthusiastic when my destination is unclear. Without a target to aim for, I become a wandering vagabond.

It is easy to get excited about traveling or beginning a new project, but when things get rough we need to make sure we are headed for a goal. Journeys are just a part of the entire adventure. Life being the definitive adventure, begins with us all starting a journey towards a destination. This destination may adjust or be reevaluated as the journey progresses, but we all must have goals in mind.

Now, our goals and destinations can change continually. Even the act of beginning a journey can force us to refocus and adjust our goals and aspirations. The key is to remember that there is joy and excitement in not only the journey but in reaching the destination.

So which one is more important? You cannot have one without the other. I would say that the journey and the destination are both essential for progress.

Zig Ziglar says, "If you aim at nothing, you will hit it every time." So without a goal, it is impossible to reach it. It sounds like common sense, but how many of us truly understand the meaning?

If you lived in New York and decided you wanted to see the Pacific Ocean, would you just hop in your car and head westward? Of course not! You would spend some time devising a strategy and choosing a location as your destination. Yes, you might adjust the trip schedule along the way for landmarks and bathroom breaks, but you would never set out on an adventure without some sort of destination in mind.

What Mr. Ziglar is praising is the forethought and planning that needs to be done before beginning a journey. The end goal is very important, but it often evolves and becomes refined. Don't get too bogged down on a finite goal. We need to leave room for improvement and be adaptable. These large goals are important, but at the very least you need to set the direction. Setting a course in the general location you want to be is better than not planning at all. Setting the direction is essential before any steps forward can begin. It allows you to start the journey even if you only have vague inklings of where you want to end up.

When I was just out of college and dating the woman who is now my wife, we decided to head out on a camping trip. We packed up my car with all the gear we expected to use: tents, sleeping bags, hiking gear, and all the necessities for a weekend in the wilderness. We knew which state park we wanted to stay at and mapped the route. After several hours in the car we arrived at the gates of the state park. We parked and headed into the ranger station to get our campsite assignment. This is where some planning would have saved me a lot of embarrassment in front of the woman I was trying to woo. They were booked. Totally booked. There was not a single campsite available in the entire park! I was pretty crestfallen.

Knowing that we wanted to hike in this particular state park, we found alternative accommodations. As it turns out, we stayed at a very questionable Super 8 Motel on the highway we drove in on, and because of our excitement, the trip was still very enjoyable. We may have had to adjust our plans, but since we had chosen our destination we were able to keep the end goal within reach. We were still able to day hike through the park, and it made for a cute story about how I failed to plan ahead.

The key point here is that as long as we have a target and maintain our enthusiasm, we can handle any issues that we encounter.

There is much adventure to be had, but setting the destination (goal) makes sure we are aiming in the right direction. You can always change the goal or time frame once the journey has begun, but beginning with the end in mind will keep you tracking in the right direction.

Without knowing where you want to be, how can you develop a plan to get there?

We all need a target, a goal to hit as proof that our efforts were valuable. Enthusiasm is no different. We must know the goal of our enthusiasm and aim for it. We can be unrestrained in how we apply and adjust our positive energy, but we must have a target, and we mustn't be idle.

Enthusiasm without action is useless. You must have a way to channel the enthusiasm.

Motivation is enough to get started, but to reach your goals you must take action!

Exercises:

- Think of a time when you adjusted your plans to account for unforeseen circumstances. Did this change the end goal?

- How were your priorities affected from this change in plans?

- Did you welcome the challenge, or did you let these setbacks interfere with your attitude? In hindsight, how could you have approached that situation differently?

- What Goals do you have right now? Are they scheduled, measurable, and attainable?

Chapter 9
From Tom Sawyer to Wedding Usher:
Being Accountable

We have talked about the responsibilities and
overcoming the frustrations that come with being
enthusiastic. Another point I would like to make is that
having enthusiasm makes you truly accountable! Ok,
that sounds a bit grandiose, but it's true. Having
excitement and energy behind a message is great, as long
as you understand that you are accountable for the
repercussions.

What do you think of when you hear the word accountability? Does it imply liability, fault, or responsibility? We all understand that it is important to be accountable for our own actions, but sometimes we are accountable for the actions of others.

In many situations, I often find myself asking "Am I accountable for this?" If that question crosses my mind, then I know that I am usually accountable in some way.

In business, as in life, it is not enough to know that we are responsible for our own actions. We are expected to maintain an understanding of how other people's accountability, or lack of accountability, can affect our own goals and aspirations.

It is easy to forget how accountable we really are when we get too excited or overly enthusiastic.

Enthusiasm can be infectious; it can spread and be used to invoke great attitudes and actions. It is a wonderful thing as long as this power is used for good.

Once, I was asked to be in usher at my cousin's
wedding. It was a fairly extravagant, expertly planned
outdoor ceremony. The chairs were lined up nicely in
rows, the arboretum was ready for the happy couple's
nuptials, and the guests were anticipating a beautiful
event. An hour before the wedding, storms started
moving in. Everyone was frantically checking the
weather and rushing to see if we could move the entire
ceremony indoors. They began moving chairs towards
the banquet hall in anticipation. I decided to check the
weather radar and the storms were definitely headed in
our direction. Though it was a bit foreboding, it looked
to me like the storms might hold off for a bit longer.
Being the optimist that I am, I turned to the other usher
and exclaimed "Looks likes the storms are going to hold
off just long enough for the wedding! Awesome, Huh?! I
bet they could still have it outside!" It was at this
moment that I realized the mother of the groom had

overheard me. She took my enthusiasm and optimism as an assurance that the ceremony could continue outdoors. She turned and addressed the entire crowd, "Put everything back on the grass! Josh just told me the storms will miss us!" I was mortified. All the chairs were brought back to their rows on the lawn and the ceremony commenced as planned, under the ominous threat of heavy rain. During the wedding, my eyes were glued to the sky. I worried that my overly enthusiastic, private discussion with the other usher might be responsible for ruining this wedding. I was seriously accountable for the decisions that were made and I would be held at fault once the skies opened up. Luckily, the storm held off just long enough. Had we not been so fortunate, I would've been wholly responsible for the calamity.

We need to be aware of how our excitement can influence those around us. It is very easy to have our intentions misunderstood. We have to be accountable.

Have you ever been caught up in the pure excitement of someone else's enthusiasm? It can happen quite easily, especially if the person is charismatic. It is a natural tendency of humans to join in the excitement of others. When someone is speaking with a great deal of passion, you will often find yourself nodding in agreement. When you recognize someone's genuine enthusiasm it is not difficult to take on their position as your own. We like to fit in, especially when we are compelled by positive emotional rhetoric.

I recall being a teenager and wrapping people's trees and houses with toilet paper. Now did I set out to roam the neighborhood and be mischievous? Of course not. It was a fellow teen who talked me into it. Now, we could chalk it up to peer pressure, and on some level I am sure it was, but looking back at it now, the reason I wanted to go along with it was because I became excited about it. My friend was very excited to go wrap houses, and his enthusiasm made me excited. I was motivated by his energy to join in the activity. There was no guilt trip that made me go along, and it wasn't the fact that I wanted to look cool. The reason I wanted to wrap houses with my friend was because his enthusiasm made me excited.

As a bit of justice, I recall having to clean up toilet paper from one neighbor's house after one of these episodes. I was forced to be accountable for my actions on this occasion, though in reality I probably should have been disciplined more harshly.

Examples like this show how easy it is to enlist others into your cause with enthusiasm. Inciting action in others is a very powerful skill, but the motivations must be benevolent or you are just using people for personal gain. Manipulation for self-interest should never be the goal of enthusiasm. Remember Tom Sawyer talking others into whitewashing the fence? He was just using his enthusiasm to convince others to do his chores. Though his cunning is impressive, in the end it was just manipulation. What about someone who uses their enthusiasm to coerce others to pick on the new kid? Or when someone convinces their peers to join in on some vandalism? It's is easy to see how misplaced energy can take a wrong turn and end up influencing people in a negative way.

We have to be personally accountable for how our excitement affects others. It's great to motivate, but it's bad to manipulate!

Disclaimer:

Throughout history, people with great presence and energy have used their influence to dictate, coerce, and manipulate.

In leadership roles it is very important to motivate and inspire. What needs to be understood is that inspiring a team is not the same as manipulating them. Tricking people into carrying out your will is not acceptable. Forcing people to do your bidding is villainous. Our enthusiasm and our passion must be used to share our genuine excitement for positive outcomes.

Exercises:

- When was the last time you were influenced by someone else's enthusiasm?

- Have you ever been accountable for someone else's actions?

- Name a time when your enthusiasm or excitement has led to unintended consequences. Was the outcome good or bad?

Chapter 10
Lemonade, Gas Pedals, and Steve Jobs:
Productivity in Relation to Enthusiasm

Enthusiasm, when utilized correctly, can help
individuals and teams become much more productive.
When people have a specific goal and the motivation to
reach it, obstacles can fade to the background,
turbulence softens, and all that remains is the desire to
succeed. This is the reason that motivation is so
important. When energy can be focused on the right
message, it can have an exponentially greater impact.

108

Enthusiasm can provide that little extra nudge to help overcome a roadblock. When things seem stuck or futile, our energy can help us rise to the challenge and persevere.

Have you ever had one of those days where everything you do seems to flow naturally? When time seems to be more nebulous but tasks seem easily surmountable? Most of us have experienced the feeling of running on all cylinders. We feel more productive and retain a clear understanding of our objectives as well as a knowledge of how to achieve them.

Many times, we can get caught up in these moments and just sprint with them through their duration without considering the cause. They become fleeting and are genuinely difficult to observe, let alone prolong or recreate. If you were to see it from outside your own involvement, it might seem practically superhuman.

This heightened understanding and super efficiency of our minds is very difficult to pinpoint, but the root cause can be linked to focus, deep, unobstructed focus. This sort of awareness can raise our performance and increase our overall productivity. There are many factors that go into reaching this epitome of efficiency, one of which is the energy to sustain this level of aptitude. When we focus our enthusiasm towards a goal, the results can be extraordinary. You may even surprise yourself with how high functioning you can be.

Enthusiasm should not only be used as a tool to motivate ourselves but also to help us inspire others to become more productive. When our energy is focused, we do not see the obstacles that lie in our paths. We see our targets. We can find it easier to visualize our goals and to share that vision with others. Enthusiasm is quite powerful, and when focused correctly it can manifest great things.

When I was a child, summers provided me and the other neighborhood kids with a lot of freedom. One day in particular, one of my friends came up with the brilliant idea that we should open a lemonade stand. Skeptical at first, we listened intently. He told us how we could get all the materials cheap (from our parents' pantries) and that we could evenly split all the money made. Our excitement began to swell as our little minds were filled with the prospect of having a handful of cash at the end of the day. We began talking about how and what would be required for this venture. First off, lemonade was a necessity, along with disposable cups, and the ever-important sign that read, "Lemonade 25 cents." We set everything up on a card table taken from my parents' garage. We were open for business! After a half hour of standing round without a single sale, we realized we weren't getting the traffic we anticipated; it turns out that a cul-de-sac is a horrible location for a drive-through business. No outlet means no passing cars, which means no business. It was a huge hole in our business plan! With the initial enthusiasm wearing off, our friend chimed back in, "Lets make another sign and have one of us hold it at the cross street! They can send cars down to the stand and we can have the cups ready! We'll probably get more business than we can handle!" Brilliant! Of course! How could we have missed it? This was the plan that would rocket our lemonade stand into the black. His plan worked. We began selling a lot of lemonade! Business was booming and we were taking turns pouring and collecting the money. All of a sudden the lemonade was gone. "We're out!" We had three cars waiting; how could we be so careless? We had to get more lemonade ASAP! Knowing the situation was dire, we sprinted to our homes and ran back minutes later with all the ingredients needed. In the history of mankind, this may have been the fastest that lemonade was ever mixed. The lemonade flowed once more. The execution of getting more supplies was flawless. I chalk the efficiency and rapid collaboration up to the fact we had a common goal. We all wanted to make the lemonade stand a success. We all knew what needed to be done, and we did it. We had a focus for our efforts and were able to use our energy to be quite productive. At the end of the day, we each walked away with several dollars in quarters and a huge sense of satisfaction for a job well done.

It is amazing how productive people can be when they collaborate and when they focus their efforts. Unfocused energy, however, can be very difficult to reign in. Without guide-wires in place, it is easy to expend much of our energy and still not make progress. This ties back to setting a direction to channel your enthusiasm. We must keep our goals in mind if we are to rise to the apex of our abilities and to inspire others to reach their own.

Imagine hitting the gas pedal in a car without having your hands on the wheel. There would be much energy expended and very little progress made. In fact, you very likely would end up burning out the tires or wrecking the vehicle. This is how we have to look at our energy: it is something to be harnessed and utilized, not something to be released.

Energy can set a pace, but direction sets the course. When these things work in conjunction, we can increase our productivity immensely. With an end goal in mind, it allows us to exploit our energy and look for innovative ways to be more efficient in our efforts.

Enthusiasm can have a huge effect on our productivity in our careers as well. Once during a trade show, the company I was working for decided to ship everything to the conference center ahead of time. This was our most important show of the year and all our potential clients would be there.

There was an anticipation and energy with our entire team for the days leading up to the event. We arrived at the convention center and our booth was already set up.

Everything seemed to be unfolding as planned until we were looking to stock the brochure stands. Where was the box of marketing material?! Where were all our pamphlets and white papers? We looked throughout the booth and we could not find a single piece of marketing material.

All of us knew this was a critical situation. We had 15 hours until the show floor opened and our prospective clients would be wandering by our booth. We had to act quickly! Luckily, our operations manager took the reigns. He acknowledged this was an inconvenience, but he expected this to be our best trade show yet! He got us excited about rising to this challenge and began delegating tasks that would resolve the problem.

With the address of a local printing company that agreed to stay open late, I headed out. At the same time, our marketing team scrambled to identify and send over the correct material to be printed. Everyone was working towards this common goal with a very high level of energy. Anyone who has worked a trade show knows that getting all your marketing material completed hours before the show can be a very difficult task. With expert direction and an enthusiastic execution, we were able to have everything ready by time the conference doors opened. Our enthusiasm helped us focus on the immediate issue and develop quick solutions. Our marketing and sales team had never been so productive in such a short amount of time.

Having a common goal and the support of those around you can lead to unstoppable enthusiasm and increased productivity.

Enthusiasm can truly have a huge impact on a person's productivity. When someone is excited, their energy directly translates to an increase in the rate at which they work. Just like listening to upbeat music when running, it sets a quicker pace and helps to develop momentum and cadence. Not only does enthusiasm affect someone's personal productivity, it can influence those in close proximity as well. Working with someone who has energy and is more productive can inspire people to rise to their level of energy. Enthusiastic people can act as a catalyst in a group environment.

Steve Jobs was asked "Why are you so successful at Apple?" Steve answered with, "We're just enthusiastic about what we do."

We are just enthusiastic? In all the things that he could have attributed his success in cutting edge technology, he chose to highlight the importance of enthusiasm.

Anyone would agree that Steve Jobs had a passion for his work and an insatiable drive to succeed. He explored uncharted territory and convinced others of his vision. How did he create one of the most productive, innovative, and successful technology companies in the world?: through his enthusiasm. He knew that having a team that was passionate towards a common goal was paramount to their success. To be productive they had to desire it, and they had to be inspired to put in the extra effort.

Not only did Steve Jobs use his enthusiasm to ensure his company's productivity, he used his enthusiasm to motivate and to lead.

Exercises:

- Name three daily activates you could do that would add energy to your efforts throughout the day.

- What impact would doing these activities have on your productivity? Would you complete more tasks? Would you have more time for other endeavors?

- I challenge you to add these three activities to your daily routine for one week and assess their impact.

Chapter 11
Naps, Moving trucks, and Leaders:
Leading through Enthusiasm

You get the best effort from others not
by lighting a fire beneath them, but by
building a fire within. –Bob Nelson

All true leaders have enthusiasm. Whether you are
leading your family through an airport, leading an
expedition to the summit of Mt. Everest, or leading a
new project team in an office, enthusiasm is the best way
to obtain and retain support from those around you.

Leaders need enthusiasm to get others to follow them.
However, being a leader is not the same as being bossy
or being someone's manager. Managers give directives
and pass down marching orders. They are more likely to

tell someone what to do instead of teaching them how to do it. In our personal lives, these types of people are often the ones who could be heard uttering "Do as I say, not as I do." In the business world, many times these managers will be in their offices emailing out bureaucratic responses and cc'ing enough people to cover their tail and limit liability. In direct opposition, leaders pick up the banner and run ahead, urging the people around them to follow. These people lead through inspiration and through generating enthusiasm within their team.

Leaders seek to help others understand the objectives before asking people to follow their direction. Managers just want people to do what they are told. We've all heard parents give the "Because I said so," explanation to their children. As this is sometimes necessary because children have not developed reasoning skills, it rings a very sour note for anyone who has spent too much time being fed these types of phrases. People who retain this type of attitude (outside of handling young children) do not appreciate how motivation and leadership could make their efforts much easier. It's much easier and much more fulfilling to convince people that your cause is worth their support. Whether it is leading your friends to a new restaurant or being the captain a soccer team, people would much rather please a leader than take orders from a manager.

In the business world, we all recognize differences in how people with authority wield it. It becomes clear that managers have employees, and leaders have team members. Which type do you think works harder for their respective companies? Who is personally invested emotionally and psychologically? Leaders earn respect, while managers take authority.

The same goes in our personal lives. Let's say that I am going to be hosting some people over to my home in the evening. What would be the best way to get my family to help me clean up? I guarantee that if I begin barking orders at them, they will complain and fight me the entire evening. However, if I begin cleaning up myself and get them excited about the end result, they will be much more willing to help. No one likes to be bossed around, but people love to be part of a team. If someone can be motivated and truly made to feel valuable, they will go above and beyond for the people who enlisted their help.

A main character trait that often sets leaders apart is their enthusiasm. People who can motivate others are more likely to advance in life and in business. And what better way to motivate others than through being enthusiastic?

Have you ever met someone who was so passionate, so enthusiastic that you couldn't help but take up their plight as your own? These people are very rare in business environments, but many can be found working in philanthropic roles. Why? It's quite simple; it is because people feel more at ease being overtly energetic and passionate about selfless causes. We are often skeptical of people who are overly enthusiastic about their business. Volunteers and philanthropists, on the other hand, have an excuse for being enthusiastic. They are given a pass because they have a cause and are allowed to motivate and incite others into action.

I suggest that we take this same energy and excitement and apply it to all other aspects of our lives. As I've said before, to be genuinely enthusiastic about something you must believe in it. And if you truly believe in something, why would you not have passion for it? Don't be ashamed of your enthusiasm! Embrace it; share it.

Have you ever worked for someone who is apathetic and/or complacent? I have. There have been several times in my working life where the people in charge of managing and motivating the team just didn't care.

One job stands out as a great example. When I was in high school, I worked for a truck rental and storage facility where we rented out moving trucks of varying sizes. My first day on the job, I noticed that many of the other employees were lounging around quite blatantly. When I asked if it was a slow time for our business, they said no. They affirmed that they had quite a lot of work to get done, but they just "didn't have the time." Didn't have the time? To put it bluntly, these people were unmotivated and lazy. There was ample time for them to address the laundry list of things they needed to get done, but they were just too apathetic. They didn't care. My next thought was "How could these people still be employed here?" Well, I soon got my answer when the manager showed up at 10:30 am, even though we opened at 8. Not only that, he took a two-hour lunch and napped in his car for part of the afternoon. I was confused at first, but over next few weeks, it was easy to fall victim to this lazy mindset that was endorsed by the manager. Trucks remained unwashed and unmaintained.

Our sales numbers were way down. It seemed that the only time people were really motivated to work hard was before corporate management planned to visit our site. On those days, everyone would work tirelessly for a few hours to make the shop look presentable. We, though I hesitate to include myself in this group, were being very reactionary. No one wanted to do any of the work and we took action only when absolutely necessary.

The morale at this job was dismal, and the work ethic was appalling. Over the coming weeks, I was slowly lulled into thinking this sort of mentality was acceptable. I had lost my zeal and enthusiasm because of the careless nature of my manager. How on earth could I be excited about being at work if my manager couldn't care less?

Luckily, this job ended when I went off to college, but the reality of the situation was not lost on me. Those people were in a dead end job because they made it a dead end job. Their lack of enthusiasm perpetuated their attitude and their position in life. For me, this was a great example of how important it is to stay motivated and to surround yourself with motivated people.

In direct opposition to that story, some people (leaders) I have had the pleasure of reporting to were fantastic! Their goal was to provide a palpable energy to the office.

People smiled broader when they came in just because they knew that their positive attitude was going to brighten the day. One particular leader would take an interest in what each member of our team was working on, and even more fascinating, was how he managed to make each person feel valued for their efforts. He strived to show people how their work and their emotional engagement at the office was truly appreciated. He would get so enthusiastic about our projects that everyone would get wrapped up in the excitement. There were days when I would be so enthusiastic about our projects that we would end up working late without even noticing. His enjoyment shined so brightly that it spread to the entire team. His motivation and tireless energy was a driving factor for all of our team's accomplishments. He truly led through enthusiasm. Everyone wanted to work harder for him. He didn't apply himself partially; he was truly invested in the success of each of us and success of the company. To this day, his positive attitude and his enthusiasm are still helping others to achieve great goals.

The people we spend time with, especially the people we take direction from, have a huge impact on our own personal attitude. Leading with enthusiasm applies to our personal lives as well. It is fairly rare to have clear leadership roles in our personal and social lives. Many times, a collective democracy is in charge when we make group decisions. However, enthusiasm can play a huge role in these situations as well. People tend to look for positive leadership and direction. Everyone wants a reason to get excited.

Many times, we dismiss the amount of influence our surroundings have on our emotions. However, enthusiasm starts with those in leadership roles: our parents, our bosses, and managers. Whether they know it or not, these people wield great power. When they get excited, it can be very infectious. Their energy has the ability to change others emotional state in bold ways. People want to rally around a common goal because we desire that camaraderie and the motivation that comes with it.

If you are leading, recognize how impactful your attitude and demeanor can be. When it comes to leading through enthusiasm, mediocrity is not an option. It's not enough to be motivated; others need to see you as their source of motivation, and it's not enough to be inspired, you have to be inspirational. People have a deep desire to be led well. They need motivation in the form of energy and positive thinking.

It is not necessary for someone to be in a formal position

of power in order to motivate and inspire others. Many people have unofficial leaders who they look to for advice and support. Many times it is the people who we work with directly who strengthen our enthusiasm and drive us to succeed.

Great leaders know how to use their enthusiasm to inspire great things from their team. They have an energy that excites others, and these leaders desire others to become passionate as well. Enthusiasm has a magnetic attraction that draws people in, and it is an inherent quality in natural born leaders.

Exercises:

- Who is the one person who motivates you more than anyone else?

- Name three ways a leader has inspired you to work harder?

- What are three ways you will lead (formally or informally) through enthusiasm this week?

Chapter 12

House Hunting and Cookies Before Bed:

What do you Risk for Being Enthusiastic?

> *For every opportunity you miss because*
> *you're too enthusiastic, you will miss a*
> *hundred more because you're not*
> *enthusiastic enough! –Zig Ziglar*

More is gained through being enthusiastic than through
being skeptical and/or quiet.

By showing excitement and enthusiasm, what do you
risk?

One might argue that you risk people not taking you
seriously. Ok, fair point.

Not being taken seriously could definitely be a drawback

when being over-enthusiastic, but only if you are blindly getting excited about something. When you place naive energy behind anything you risk the possibility of looking foolish. However, focused enthusiasm will probably not cause you to lose credibility.

It may not surprise you that I have almost never been accused of being too serious. Too immature? Yes. Too carefree? Yes. Too excitable? Yes.

So the risk of not being taken seriously never weighed that heavily on my mind. I often get very excited about things to the point where it overwhelms others. To me, it is more important to be enthusiastic about something than to be taken seriously. The energy that is put into supporting something will only rarely detract from the end goal. So why not be enthusiastic?

What I am trying to convey to you is that enthusiasm can't hurt! You get to decide to be engaged!

You will almost never lose anything by showing enthusiasm. In fact, not being enthusiastic could end up costing you a lot, whether it's a family outing, a special project, a promotion at the office, or even just recognition for a job well done. Not only do people appreciate the energy that someone shows, this enthusiasm can spread to others.

People with determination and passion tend to succeed more often than those who are indifferent. No one wants to do business with someone who's boring.

Going to work and doing the bare minimum of what is expected of you will only help you keep a job. However, doing things with energy and excitement will help you build a career and possibly prepare you for a more important role.

How do you define risk? Essentially, risk is the danger of exposure in one form or fashion. But if we look at it personally, what is risky to us? Are we risking our livelihood or possibly our reputation? Are we risking the good opinions people have about us? Are we risking our family's well-being? Risking death? Of course not! These are drastic extremes that help to illustrate how easy it is to let the fear get in the way of progress and excitement. There is risk associated with most things in life. Each day, we take many risks. Some risks are unconscious, and other risks are conscious and calculated, but no matter what, we all have to take risks. Think about it, how much thought did you put into the risks associated with driving your car today? Is there risk there? Yes, but it doesn't mean we have to be fearful and nervous.

A great example of risk being measured incorrectly comes from a personal interaction I had with a colleague who was in the market for a new house. He and his wife had excitedly looked at quite a few homes and had even had a contract on two properties. However, both these properties fell through due to unresolvable issues that came up during the inspections. So they continued their search. Eventually, he and his wife found a great home that filled the majority of their wish list. Around this time we had a conversation about how his home search was going. His reply was almost depressing. He said, "I found a house that fits my needs, but we would have to negotiate and then do the inspection, but who knows, I might not even make the offer."

He seemed practically dejected at the opportunity in front of him. I understand that having a couple setbacks can be disheartening, but this person sounded defeated. He sounded like he had already thrown in the towel before he started trying to buy this house. He didn't want to risk putting his emotions on the line. I inquired further about what the house was like. He described a new kitchen, updated baths, and a large yard. To me this sounded pretty nice, so I responded with "Wow, that sounds pretty great, are you excited about this house?" He replied "No, I'm not excited, yet; I think I might be if we get past all this stuff and once we get to the closing. After all the issues with the other houses, I doubt this one is going to pan out."

Again, I understand being a bit disappointed that the several homes didn't get past the inspection. It's understandable that someone would be a bit cautious, but the sad attitude that this person was harboring was pathetic. He was running down all the possible outcomes for what could go wrong before he even reached them. It's great to be prepared and to have contingency plans, but to let this fear take the excitement and enjoyment out of a purchasing a new home is going too far. He had lost his original enthusiasm about house hunting and it had been replaced by cynical distrust. This is no way to live!

He let his fear of risking emotional investment keep him from being excited. His downtrodden attitude was holding him back from taking action and from being optimistic about the potential opportunity that was directly in front of him.

I think everyone would agree that attitude makes a huge difference. If your attitude is enthusiastic, others will see you as someone who is better than the rest of the herd. Today, it is very easy to stand out as a go getter in environments that are plagued by apathy.

Have you ever wondered why people can be promoted if they are not as skilled or smart as others? It's because enthusiasm and the ability to incite excitement in others is a highly valued personality trait. In many ways, it is more valuable than knowledge and expertise.

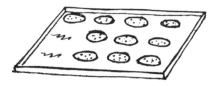

Like many children, I loved snacks before bed. Especially sweets. Many times I would plead my case for a snack, and on occasion my parents would cave.

When I was about 9 years old, I remember one particular evening. Things were winding down and I knew my parents would soon be telling me to head upstairs and brush my teeth before bed. Suddenly, I remembered that my mother had made dozens of chocolate chip cookies earlier that day, the kind that were laden with chocolate morsels, with just the right amount of softness. This became my mission before bed: acquire cookies. I was very excited about this potential pre-bedtime snack and went to ask my mother. I excitedly walked up to her and enthusiastically asked "Can I have two cookies before bed?!" Even as a child I understood the need to leave room for negotiation; settling at one cookie was still better than none. True to my expectations, my energetic request for two cookies was met with a stern "No, you may have one." Still very excited, I replied "Ok, great!" and turned to walk towards the kitchen. Then my mother stopped me and gave me a lesson that has stayed with me well into adulthood. She said "You know what? Since you were so happy and respectful of my decision, you can have two cookies."

I was beside myself with awe and excitement. I couldn't believe that just being happy could have such an amazing result.

This lesson taught me that the mere act of being

enthusiastic and excited cannot work against you. Is it going to yield that second cookie every time? No, but sometimes it does, and that makes it all worth it. This is applicable to so many facets of our lives.

So, why would anyone not want to be passionate or show their excitement? What possible risk could there be in showing enthusiasm? There is practically no risk in being enthusiastic. It's practically all upside!

You just need to make sure it's genuine.

Exercises:

- Name a time when you chose not to be enthusiastic because of previous setbacks.

- Did your lack of excitement affect your attitude about the final result? Did it affect the emotions of those around you?

- Challenge yourself to choose one thing that you will risk being enthusiastic about this week.

Chapter 13
PowerPoint, Believers, and Charlie Brown's Teacher:
Inspiration takes Personal Investment

What better way to inspire people than through enthusiasm?

Inspiration and enthusiasm go hand in hand, but is important to make the distinction between them.

Inspiration is when people have been moved by something or someone in a positive way. Enthusiasm is a method of conveying excitement and can incite inspiration in others.

Both these terms take a commitment and an emotional investment.

No one can expect to be inspired or enthusiastic about something until they have taken on the cause personally. Too often, we see people peddling ideas or canned dogmas when it is quite evident they do not believe in what they are saying. Anyone can convey a message loudly or even dramatically, but without being personally invested, it is impossible convey true, genuine excitement. The best way to become enthusiastic and incite inspiration in others is to truly believe what we are doing and what we're saying. I asked this in a previous chapter, "Do you have to believe in something to show enthusiasm?" Quite simply, yes. You must be committed and authentic in your efforts if you want to be truly enthusiastic. People are too smart to fall for fake enthusiasm. It is not always easy to spot a person who puts up a facade of support, but most the time it is evident if someone truly believes in their efforts.

Personal investment makes the difference between a charlatan and a devoted leader.

This personal investment is necessary for anyone to believe in what you are saying enough to take action.

Personal investment is a two-way street. You can't expect others to be excited and enthusiastic about your cause if you don't show the same energy.

Have you ever listened to someone give a presentation that lacked energy? One that was so lackluster and monotone that people in the audience were falling asleep? I have, as I'm sure you have too. It's almost painful to sit through.

Once, while I was working for a company in the software industry, I had an epiphany about the broad spectrum with which someone can convey an idea. We all know that some topics are always going to be more interesting and intriguing than others. I bet almost anyone would rather sit through a presentation on "International Kidnapping Evasion" than one about

"Company Email Protocol." However, I'm not talking about what content is better. I want to highlight how enthusiasm can make the difference between the mediocre and the fascinating. Lucky for me, I was able to see the same topic presented in two vastly different styles. The topic?: "Standard contracts and our legal terms and conditions." Yeah, email protocol doesn't look that bad anymore, does it? Anyway, this topic was originally presented by one of our lawyers during a company-wide web-based PowerPoint presentation. The lawyer covered topics like why we need contracts, who's at risk for unsigned terms, indemnification, government regulations on software sales, and proprietary development. It was so soul-crushingly, mind-numbingly boring that I wanted to cry and was one of the most brutally monotone, lethargy-inducing presentations I have ever seen. To this person's credit, I am sure his information was accurate. He stated everything in a matter-of-fact manner. There was no emotion or energy behind his words. It was death by PowerPoint and no one could escape. With his lack of intonation, he sounded like Ferris Bueller's teacher. Yes, this person had an appreciation for details, but by the time I saw the 7th slide in a row with more than 15 bullet points, I checked out. At that point, his words turned into the "Wah wah wah" of Charlie Brown's teacher. I can hardly fault anyone for not paying attention after that point. I wanted to stay focused, and I'm sure there was some very important information that I missed, but my attention could not be held any longer.

About a month later we had a new head council brought in to run our legal group. He asked to speak on this same topic during our annual sales and technical training week. No one was excited. It was bad enough to sit through it once, but a second time? Please say it isn't so! This had to be in breach of the Geneva Convention!

Luckily for everyone in the audience, his approach was entirely different. When he began his presentation, he was able to sincerely emote an excitement for the topic. In his first couple sentences he referenced the fact that this is not a fun thing to listen to, but he would make it as enjoyable as possible. Right off the bat, he appealed to our sense of humor with a couple good lawyer jokes. You could hear his enthusiasm in every sentence that was spoke. He made lighthearted comments about the topic of contracts. He used funny pictures as analogies. He hit the high points of what was applicable to us as an audience, and he presented the entire thing with an air of passion. He truly enjoyed telling us about it. He had a dynamic range to how he emphasized key points and glossed over things that weren't relevant. He had captured everyone's attention through one thing, his

enthusiasm.

Quite arguably, it was the best presentation on a legal topic I have ever sat through. The reason it was so good was because of the energy and the excitement he brought with him. The topic was not predestined to be entertaining, but the enthusiastic manner in which it was presented not only captured our attention but instilled in us an appreciation and respect for the topic. He liked talking about contracts, and he was personally invested in making sure we truly cared about it as well. He engaged us during his talk, and because of his efforts, the energy he had for it spread to the audience.

What that speaker knew was that energy is infectious and that excitement can be contagious. You can take an idea, and when it's mixed with the right amount of excitement, you can drive other people's passion. You can steer their efforts into picking up the banner with you and supporting your efforts. Each of us has the ability to inspire others, and it is a huge responsibility. When we are committed to what we are saying and are energetic in how we present it to others, the message has the ability to resonate with those around us.

Inspiration without application is useless. It is not enough just to excite people. A feeling or moment of joy can be fleeting. To truly stick, enthusiasm must be absorbed and excitement must be taken personally. We have to believe in what we are doing to inspire others and we have to be personally invested to be genuinely enthusiastic.

Exercises:

- Name three things you are personally and emotionally invested in.

- On a scale from 1 to 5, how much passion do you display when you talk about each thing?

- How much passion and enthusiasm do you emote when talking about your career?

- Are these things aligned or lopsided?

Chapter 14
Where do you keep your Slingshot?
- The *Back Pocket* Theory

I briefly mentioned the **Back Pocket** theory in previous chapters, but in this one I will break it down further and really add substance to show you how it can be applied. I've called it a deeply-guarded secret for overcoming fear and anxiety. It's a recipe for becoming awesome, but it's not really a secret at all. It heavily relies on your ability to recognize the importance of things beyond what you are currently facing. You have to take the time to acknowledge that what you are worrying about is important to you, and that's why you are nervous about it. The big secret?

Well it's not really a secret after all: **YOU** are a master of your own destiny! You get to choose enthusiasm and subsequently happiness and success! It may sound ridiculous, but the most useful truths are often the simplest. Confidence and optimism can help you be enthusiastic, and enthusiasm can lead you to the happiness and success you deserve!

Right now, you must be feeling a lot like Dorothy at the end of *The Wizard of Oz*. You've gone on a long journey only to find out that you already possessed the abilities from the very beginning. To help you get over your disappointment, let me add a little more substance.

The crux of this back pocket theory is self-assurance. You have to believe in yourself! No one else is going to believe in you if you don't. If you question your own motivations and goals, it can be very difficult to use the back pocket method. You have to be comfortable in your own skin, confident in your efforts, and assured of your own intrinsic value.

It sounds like a lot of introspection is necessary, but that's not always the case. The simplest it can be put is that if you truly believe in yourself, it doesn't matter if others do. You have to be you because no one else can.

The really funny thing is, once you are not striving for others' approval, you are more likely to receive it. If your positive attitude is derived internally, others will seek to share in your happiness. It becomes an innate confidence. This confidence is something you keep in your back pocket, like Dennis the Menace's slingshot. It's right there where you can reach it if you need to.

We have to understand that our enthusiasm can tap into others' personalities. It allows us to show a resolve and persistence that can captivate those around us.

Enthusiasm has the power to overcome critics and slay our own personal insecurities. Enthusiasm allows us to keep going in the face of defeat. It helps us to continue our efforts and try even harder. Passion and excitement can have a greater impact than natural talent or intelligence. We must drive on, we have to keep trying, and we must be persistent!

> *Nothing in this world can take the place*
> *of persistence. Talent will not: nothing*
> *is more common than unsuccessful men*

*with talent. Genius will not; unrewarded
genius is almost a proverb. Education
will not: the world is full of educated
derelicts. Persistence and determination
alone are omnipotent.   -Calvin
Coolidge*

What is Mr. Coolidge trying to say? He practically
ridicules people who are talented, educated, or highly
intelligent. Why? It is not because he thinks these types
of people do not deserve success. His true intent with
this quote is that persistence and determination will take
you further than anything else. Persistence can overcome
a lack of skill. Having a deep-seated determination can
drive your success more consistently than being
intelligent. He is implying that anyone can be great if
they continually strive to. A tenacious nature can have a
huge impacts on results. We have to keep going; we
have to strive for what we want, and we have to be
confident and excited. How do we do this? With
enthusiasm. Keep in mind that you benefit more from
enthusiasm and determination than you do from actual
knowledge. Enthusiasm gives you an upper hand in
everything you do.

Staying confident when faced with opposition or
nervousness can help you rise above the mediocre. It

allows you to be the best you that you can be. Push yourself to be excited! You do not have to be talented or smart to be inspirational. You just have to choose to be enthusiastic. People are more likely to remember your energy and less likely to recall any mistakes. You can always overcome a lack of expertise as long as you are enthusiastic. I am not suggesting that you use enthusiasm as a crutch, but you should use it as a tool for inspiring those around you.

There are ways we can psych ourselves up and get excited in the moment, from listening to motivational talks and upbeat songs, to physical activity or just looking in the mirror. However, there are also many things we can do in our spare time to prepare us for being confident and enthusiastic. Self-reflection can give you the foundation for self-assuredness. Taking a few minutes every day to sit quietly and reflect can do wonders for your confidence. This type of introspective thought can not only center your focus, it can empower you to be bolder and more assertive. When people recognize others as self-reliant, it only reinforces any message presented. Being confident will enable others to have confidence in you. Acting self-assured will assure others of your abilities and value.

Nothing can stop the man with the right mental attitude from achieving his goal; nothing on earth can help the man with the wrong mental attitude." –Thomas Jefferson

It's up to you to have the right attitude and confidence. However, we all know to never put all our eggs in one basket. It's a common phrase and it has been used to describe everything from retirement investing to rooting for sports teams. In relation to the back pocket theory, knowing that you have many things that are personally important, allows you to put less weight behind any single action or interaction. Having something bigger than yourself can ease your fears and take away the pressure to perform. When the pressure is off, you are more genuine and more likable.

Every year, my elementary school would host a skate

party at the local roller skating rink, where people roller skate around in circles to music. It sounds less appealing now, but in my youth it was the place to be! Everyone from my grade was at the roller rink this particular day. We were all hanging out with our friends, playing in the arcade, skating to the music, and having too many sodas. Some of the biggest events at the rink were when they would play the slow songs. Instinctively, the girls and boys would separate and then only the bravest guys would approach the girls and ask one of them to skate around holding hands.

Hopped up on too much caffeine and adrenaline, I skated across the semi-empty rink to ask a girl that I had a crush on to skate with me. Then, in front of all her friends, she said "No." Back then, this was a pretty big deal and in hindsight it should have been much more embarrassing. However, I remember thinking "That's fine, I'd rather be playing at the arcade anyway." This small scenario could have easily been a huge emotional trauma, but I didn't let this single rejection define me. I had other things I was emotionally invested in. There was other fun to be had. I had something in my back pocket.

When you know that your entire life is not dependent on one single situation, it allows you to take more risks, to be bolder with your convictions, and to keep things in

151

perspective. When you know that you are not beholden to a specific outcome you can carry that with you in your back pocket. I am not saying that you shouldn't be committed to what you do, but you should never put any single thing in a position to break your spirit. Both in our personal lives and in our careers, we must be balanced. We all need to have perspective, and we need to keep something in our back pockets.

Exercises:

- What are three things you could do today that would provide you with confidence tomorrow?

- What are three things that you have in your back pocket?

- Write them down, look at them every morning, and carry the list with you for one week. Then, see how this changes your outlook on life.

Download a free *Back Pocket* template from our bonus materials!

http://www.enthusiasticyou.com/enthusiastic-you--bonus.html

Chapter 15
Blaze your Trail! –

Enthusiasm is yours to Manifest

How can I become more enthusiastic?

First off, you need to believe that you can be. It is imperative that you know that you have the capacity to be enthusiastic. You possess the ability to conjure this energy, but it will never happen on its own. You need to be intentional with your actions and emotions. It can take quite a bit of persistence, but with the right steps and a clear direction, enthusiasm is yours to summon. After some practice, these steps can become second nature. The road to becoming enthusiastic is not always easy when you are first trying to get there. If you start putting in the effort, over time it becomes a well-worn path. Eventually, you will recognize the landmarks along the trail and be able to quickly reach enthusiasm. With enough practice, you will be able to get there subconsciously and manifesting and sharing your enthusiasm with others will become much easier.

Here are those steps:

Set your Direction. Take time to understand your motivation to be enthusiastic and identify what you desire. What do you want to be enthusiastic about? Be specific. You may even have to write it down. It's important that you identify exactly what your goal is and where you want your desire and aspirations to take you. One of the best methods I have found is in deep reflection. Take some quiet time by yourself to clearly understand what you want to achieve.

Understand your Fear! Measure the risks you are taking. No matter what you're going to do, and no matter where you're going to place your enthusiasm, it's important that you identify and recognize your fear. Give your fear a name. If it has a name, you can bring it out into the light and attack it before it overwhelms you. In many cases, the act of writing down your fears can allow you to physically cross them off your list and emotionally let them go. We all must face our fears so that we can overcome the trials we will face with each task.

Be Optimistic. Make a conscious choice to be positive in your attitude and in your efforts. Forcing yourself to smile seems like an arbitrary facade, but studies have shown that the mere act of smiling can have great effects externally as well as internally. People who smile are not only perceived as happy by those who see them, they sound happier on the phone. Internally, it is just as useful because the act of smiling triggers a release of endorphins, which actually will make you happy and therefore more positive.

Build your Confidence. Summon your courage to commit and strive to be great. You deserve to be self assured! Every person in this world knows something you do not, but that's not my point. With this little piece of knowledge, it is easy to conclude that you have at least one piece of information that the person you are speaking to does not. How's that for confidence building? You are a little bit smarter than everyone in at least some small way. Remember that everyone puts on their pants one leg at a time. Know that you have value, and that no matter what, your attitude will matter more than your words. It's how you say it, not what you say that carries the most weight with people.

Identify your Audience. By understanding who the audience for your enthusiasm is, you can better tailor your message to inspire those around you. This gives you the upper hand by ensuring that you are properly understood in your efforts. We have all said things that we instantly regret; we cannot dwell on these things. By knowing your audience, we can better prepare and emote things in the exact manner we desire.

Have Energy! Get excited! Pump yourself up. There are many ways to get yourself in the right mindset. Physical activity can have an energy boosting effect. Run, take a brisk walk, go swimming (maybe even jump off a diving board a few times). Though physical exertion can be tiring in the short term, it can raise your energy levels over the long run. How about listening to your favorite upbeat song? Make sure it's one you can't help but nod your head to. Let the (positive) music take hold of your attitude. Is there an inspiring and energetic speech you've heard? Look it up on YouTube and channel that electricity into your own psyche. You can do it! I know you can! Or as my favorite pump-up song says, "You're the best around!"

Put something in your *Back Pocket!*

Exercises:

- Choose a task you have to complete this week.

- Dedicate yourself to applying each of these steps towards that task.

- Review how these steps affected your engagement and the success of your task.

Chapter 16
Rear-view Mirrors and the Most Enthusiastic Man in the Room

Can you be enthusiastic?

YES!

Is it a conscious choice?

YES!

Everyone can be enthusiastic and choose to head towards excitement and energy and away from lethargy and complacency. It may not always be easy, but it isn't complicated. All it takes is determination and a desire to excel. You have to put yourself out there! Look your fear right in the eyes and keep going.

You mustn't be scared! You can't allow yourself to be afraid of mistakes! We have to learn from them and move forward. Dwelling on mistakes can often be huge waste of time. Remember, that if the past were that important, the rear view mirror in your car would be as big as the windshield. Worrying about possible outcomes is inevitable. The key is to overcome these hindrances and not let them stifle your enthusiasm or your success.

No one is going to get out there and be energetic for you, so it's up to you to go out there and get it! You are responsible for creating your own energy. Each of us is called to be enthusiastic and to share this energy with others. It is a noble thing to incite passion in other people. We should all aspire to being a positive force!

I urge you to take a vested interest in what you are doing and what you want to achieve in your life. I implore you to be excited about your efforts and emit a positive energy. The world needs you to share your enthusiasm.

In life, we all strive for greatness in our own way. We all desire to do well. One way to get a jump start on the road to success is to be enthusiastic in all that you do.

Put in the effort! Expend the energy! Find a cause and sprint towards it! Everyone has the ability to be enthusiastic, but very few choose to be. Choose to be a better, happier, more energetic you!

Choose to become an Enthusiastic *You!*

I've never claimed to be the smartest man in the room, just the most enthusiastic.

We want to help you become an **Enthusiastic *You!***
There are many ways for you to develop and maintain your passion and energy!

Access to our free Enthusiasm resource library at:
http://www.enthusiasticyou.com/enthusiastic-you--bonus.html

Want help inciting Enthusiasm into your personal life or in your career? We can assist! Contact us for an Enthusiasm Consultation:
http://www.enthusiasticyou.com/contact.html

Follow us on twitter:
https://twitter.com/EnthusiasticYou

Like us on Facebook:
https://www.facebook.com/JoshMEvansAuthor

View our blog:
http://enthusiastictactics.blogspot.com

Register This book and get free updates.

Things change rapidly in the publishing world! If you register your copy of this book, we will keep you up to date about this book. PLUS, we will send you an Enthusiastic Checklist PDF.

Just visit http://enthusiasticyoubook.com

Enthusiastic *You!*

Rediscover Your Passion & Energy:
Tools For Success in Your Daily Life

by Joshua M. Evans